SYSTEM SOFTWARE
A SIMPLIFIED APPROACH

M. JOSEPH
Research Scholar,
National Institute of Technology,
Surathkal, Karnataka

FIREWALL MEDIA
(An Imprint of Laxmi Publications Pvt. Ltd.)
BANGALORE • CHENNAI • COCHIN • GUWAHATI • HYDERABAD
JALANDHAR • KOLKATA • LUCKNOW • MUMBAI • RANCHI
NEW DELHI

Published by :
FIREWALL MEDIA
(An Imprint of Laxmi Publications Pvt. Ltd.)
113, Golden House, Daryaganj,
New Delhi-110002

Phone : 011-43 53 25 00
Fax : 011-43 53 25 28

www.laxmipublications.com
info@laxmipublications.com

ISBN : 81-318-0036-9

First Edition : 2007

OFFICES

India

© **Bangalore**	080-26 61 15 61
© **Chennai**	044-24 34 47 26
© **Cochin**	0484-239 70 04
© **Guwahati**	0361-254 36 69, 251 38 81
© **Hyderabad**	040-24 75 02 47
© **Jalandhar**	0181-222 12 72
© **Kolkata**	033-22 27 37 73, 22 27 52 47
© **Lucknow**	0522-220 95 78
© **Mumbai**	022-24 91 54 15, 24 92 78 69
© **Ranchi**	0651-230 77 64

USA

Boston
11, Leavitt Street, Hingham,
MA 02043, USA

FSY-2878-095-SYSTEM SOFTWARE A SIMP. APP.
Typeset at : Kalyani Computer Services, New Delhi.

C—13432/07/01
Printed at : Sanjeev Offset Printers, Delhi.

To my son

Michael Arul Abel,

who only gives little hope to live

and to my wife

Josephine Suganya

for all her help, in running our family

CONTENTS

1. Introduction to System Software 1
2. Architecture 5
3. Operating System 28
4. Compilers 53
5. Assemblers 96
6. Macros and Macro Processors 115
7. Loaders and Linkers 129
8. Interpreters, Editors and Debuggers 141

Appendix 150

Bibliography 181

Index 183

PREFACE

This book has been written mainly for the beginners who are willing to undergo a course in "System Software". The concepts are dealt in lucid manner so as to reach the readers. The book will prove to be good aide to teachers who teach System Software. In this book the concepts are discussed with real world examples. The main purpose is to simplify the concepts of system programming.

The book follows the Intel architectures (Intel 8085, Intel 8086) to discuss all the concepts of system programming. This is the unique feature of this book. The Intel architecture is selected because the students are exposed only to these architectures in their curriculum. The students will feel convenient to learn the concepts of system programming with the help of these architectures. It does not follow any hypothetical architecture, which the students are unaware of. This is selected to make the students feel comfort. Almost all the concepts dealt herein are based on the Intel architectures only. Many example programs have been discussed and written using Intel architecture based instruction sets.

Chapter 1 gives a brief introduction about the System Software. The analogy given in this chapter will help to understand the basic ideas about the System Software. The overview of all the System Software in a computer system is explained with the help of a simple block diagram. The definitions for all the System Software are given in this chapter.

Chapter 2 gives the introduction about the architectures Intel 8085 and 8086 processors. The architecture, Instruction set, addressing modes, and programming details are addressed in detail in this chapter. Some programming examples are also given in this chapter. Some more example architectures are also given in this chapter.

Chapter 3 describes the basic concepts of the Operating system. The concepts, which are more relevant to the system programming, have been discussed in detail in this chapter.

Chapter 4 discusses all the concepts of the Compilers. The concepts are discussed in a very lucid manner, which will help a beginner to understand the concepts of the compilers in a very better way.

In fact, the whole book is written around the chapters Operating System and Compilers.

Chapter 5 discusses the concepts of the Assembler with the help of Intel 8085 and 8086 architectures. MASM and TASM assemblers are considered for the discussion. Some example programs are considered for explaining the concepts of an assembler. The design of single and two pass assemblers are also discussed in this chapter.

Chapter 6 discusses about the macros and macro processors. Many examples for macros for Intel architecture based assemblers are discussed in this chapter. Some macros in C programming language are also discussed in this chapter, which will be convenient for the readers to understand the macro concepts.

Chapter 7 discusses the basic concepts of loader and also its types. The design of loaders is also discussed. The design of linking loader and concepts about the linkage editor are also addressed well in this chapter.

Chapter 8 gives the details about the Editors and Debuggers. Some real editors and debuggers are discussed in this chapter.

The Appendix A gives the practical implementation of an assembler. The source code in C Language is given here. This will help the learners to understand design of an assembler and also they can come to know what a System Software implementation is.

Questions are given at the end of every chapter. Many of the questions have been asked in various universities. Questions have been categorised in Part A and Part B for the convenience of students.

—Author

ACKNOWLEDGEMENT

I am much grateful to Laxmi Publications (P) Ltd., New Delhi, for giving me an opportunity to work with them. I am also thankful to the editors and other persons of Laxmi Publications, who worked with in carrying out this venture.

I am much grateful to the Chairperson of Periyar Maniammai Institute of Science and Technology, Tanjavur, Tamil Nadu, Dr. K. Veeramani, for giving enough inspiration to come to this level.

I am very much happy to express my gratitude to the Principal of Periyar Maniammai College of Technology, Tanjavur, Tamil Nadu, Dr. N. Ramachandran, for his constant encouragement and support throughout my career and especially in this venture.

I am very much happy to express my gratitude to the Principal of National College of Engineering, Koil Patty, Tamil Nadu, Dr. Kn.K.S.K. Chockalingam for his constant encouragement and support throughout my life.

I am very much happy to express my gratitude to Dr. K. Chandra Sekaran, Professor, National Institute of Technology, Karnataka, for giving the foreword to this book.

I am also thankful to my wife A. Josephine Suganya, for helping in typing the manuscript and also her other helps in carrying out this task.

I am also thankful to my student Praveen for helping me preparing the diagrams and typing manuscript of this book.

I would like to thank my mother Mrs. S. Arockia Mary and my family members for their support throughout my life in writing related works.

I am very much grateful to Prof. M. Maria Louis, for giving me an opportunity to take up teaching as my career.

I am much indebted to my father Mr. A. Maria Michael Teacher, who was completely responsible for developing me as a teaching personality.

Finally, I thank all my students without whom I am nowhere.

—Author

CHAPTER

1

INTRODUCTION TO SYSTEM SOFTWARE

Knowing what you do not know is the real beginning of wisdom—Confucius
When you sell a man a book,
You don't sell him 12 ounces of paper and ink and glue—
You sell him a whole new life—Christopher Morley.

1.1 INTRODUCTION

In this chapter we will be seeing what are system software and their functions in detail with a simple analogy.

System software support the operation of the computers. Compilers, assemblers, loaders, linkers, operating system and other similar programs are examples for system software. We can understand the concepts of system programs with a simple analogy.

Consider an elephant, which wanders in the wilderness. Somehow it is caught by a man and brought to the city. The man knows that the elephant is mammoth creature and is capable of doing jobs of man's interest. But he cannot communicate with the elephant. If he can communicate and control it, then the elephant's potentials can be utilized. He trains and makes it ready for getting work done. He has small stick like thing and through which he controls the elephant.

MAN ⟶ **STICK** ⟶ **ELEPHANT**
(User) (Controlling element) (Computer)

Fig. 1.1 Simple analogy to system software

The above analogy can be used to understand the concept of system software. The system software help in communicating and controlling the computer in getting the work done from it. The user uses the system software as the communicating and controlling element in order to get work done from the computer. The system software is dependent on the architecture of machine for which these are designed. In fact these are separate programs, which are responsible for a particular transformation of the source program. The system software can also be called as language processors.

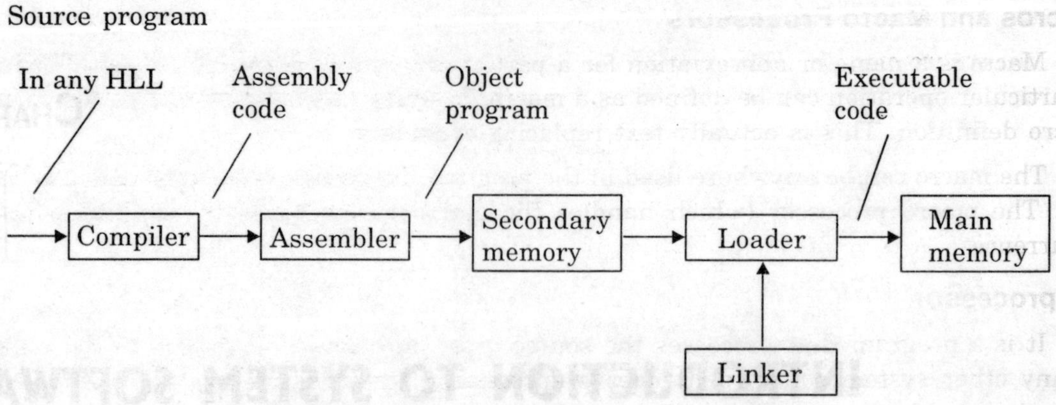

Fig. 1.2 Overview of system software in a computer

1.2 OVERVIEW OF SYSTEM SOFTWARE

The user writes the program (source program) in any High Level Language (HLL) and submits it for execution. This program undergoes various changes before it gets converted into an object program for execution. The transformations, which the source program has to undergo, are the works done by the system software. These can be explained by the help of the block diagram shown Fig. 1.2. This discussion will give the broader sketch for all the system software used in a computer.

Compilers

It is a program, which converts the source program written in any HLL into an object program. It has various phases like lexical analyzer, parser, semantic analyzer, intermediate code generator, and code optimizer and code generator. The source program undergoes transformations through all the above phases and gets converted into an object program. The code generator generates actually symbolic code, which is nothing but assembly language code (Assembly Language Program). This assembly language program can further be processed in the assembler. In fact the compiler generates assembly language code depending on the architecture of the machine.

Assemblers

Assembler is a program, which translates assembly language program into machine language program (object program). It places the object program in the secondary memory.

Loaders

Loader is a program (can be a sub program) that loads the object program from the secondary memory into the main memory during the execution of the program. Then the control is transferred to that. There are various loading schemes available like absolute, relocating and direct linking. It is sometimes called as locators.

Linkers

Linker links the necessary libraries (library routines) for execution of certain program, during the execution. It is actually a part of loader's function.

Macros and Macro Processors

Macro is a name or abbreviation for a part of program (subroutine). A set of codes for a particular operation can be defined as a macro. Defining any subroutine like this is called macro definition. This is actually text replacing capability.

The macro can be anywhere used in the program. Its occurrence can be called as macro call. The macro processor (which handles the macros) substitutes the definition in that occurrence.

Preprocessor

It is a program that processes the source program before it is passed to the compiler or any other system software. It does preprocessing functions on the source program to make it suitable for compilation. It provides convenience to the programmers.

E.g.: Macro processor.

Operating System

It is actually the manager of the machine. It allocates resources to various jobs being run in the computer. The resources may be memory, CPU time, I/O devices and others. It can be called as a resource allocator. It also controls all activities of the computer like memory management, I/O management, processor management, process management and others. So it can be called as a control program too. It is a program to allocate resources and control the activities of the computer.

Editors and Debuggers

Editors are used to create new files and modify the same. There are plenty of examples for the editors. Few examples are given below:

1. Turbo C editor
2. Vi editor
3. Note pad
4. Norton editor and
5. Others.

Debuggers are the system programs used to debug the programs. It helps the programmers to debug during the program development. *A debugger is also a system program, which allows debugging, trouble shooting any program.*

Fig. 1.3 shows an example of how a HLL code is undergoing various transformations through respective system software. The reader will understand the concepts behind these transformations after reading all the other chapters.

Summary

In this chapter we have seen what are system software and how these are responsible for carrying out the system related activities *i.e.*, the internal functions of the computer system. The over view of all the system software is also discussed. The definitions of all the system software and their functions are clearly addressed in this chapter.

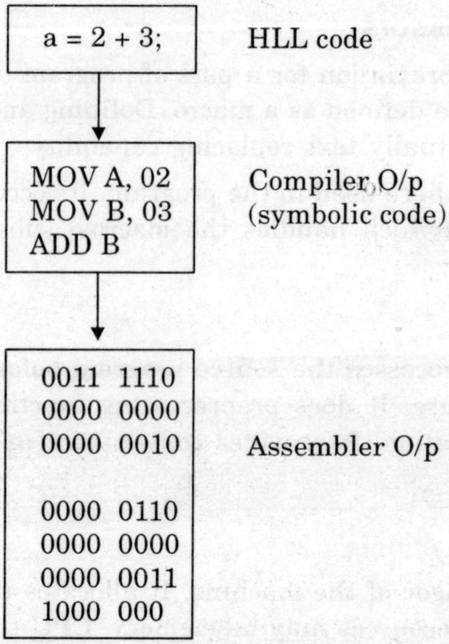

Fig. 1.3 HLL code and its transformations through system software

QUESTIONS

Part A

1. What are the types of software?
2. What is application software?
3. What is system software?
4. List some examples of system software.
5. Define system software.
6. What is a compiler?
7. What is an assembler?
8. What is a loader?
9. What is a linker?
10. What are macros and macro processors.
11. What are preprocessors; give examples.
12. Name few editors, which are popularly used.
13. What are the functions of an operating system?
14. What are preprocessors?

Part B

1. What are the transformations a program does undergo before it gets executed?
2. Discuss in detail about the over view of system software used in a computer system.

CHAPTER 2

ARCHITECTURE

Blessed are those who mourn,
For they shall be comforted.

2.1 INTRODUCTION

In this chapter we are going to discuss in detail about the architecture of a machine. This is necessary to understand the concepts of system software. Intel 8085 is considered as an example processor. This chapter mainly concentrates the details of processor, which are much necessary for writing assembly language programs since assembly language program is one essential component in the study of system software. In this section we will be discussing about the architecture, registers, instruction set, instruction formats and addressing modes pertinent to the processor 8085. Some assembly language programs are also discussed in this chapter. In this book we consider the processor 8085 because still it is worth learning the basics about a machine. We consider all the architectural details pertinent to 8085 to understand the concepts of system software. The necessary architectural details of 8086 are also discussed in this chapter. These will help in understanding the advanced features of assemblers.

2.2 8085 MICROPROCESSOR

Microprocessor is a Large Scale Integrated Chip, which can be programmed to do the tasks of our interest. The architectural details can be understood with the help of the following diagram Fig. 2.1.

Buses

Group of wires for carrying binary information can be called as bus. The 8085 processor has address bus, data bus, and control bus and each one carry its own type of information.

Address Bus

This is used to carry the address of data, instruction, *i.e.*, memory word in general. This is unidirectional (carries information in one way only). In Intel 8085 processor the address bus length is 16 bits. The total addressable memory can be 2^{16}. This will be 65536. This can be also called 64 K bytes. One K byte is 2^{10} bits *i.e.*, 1024 bits.

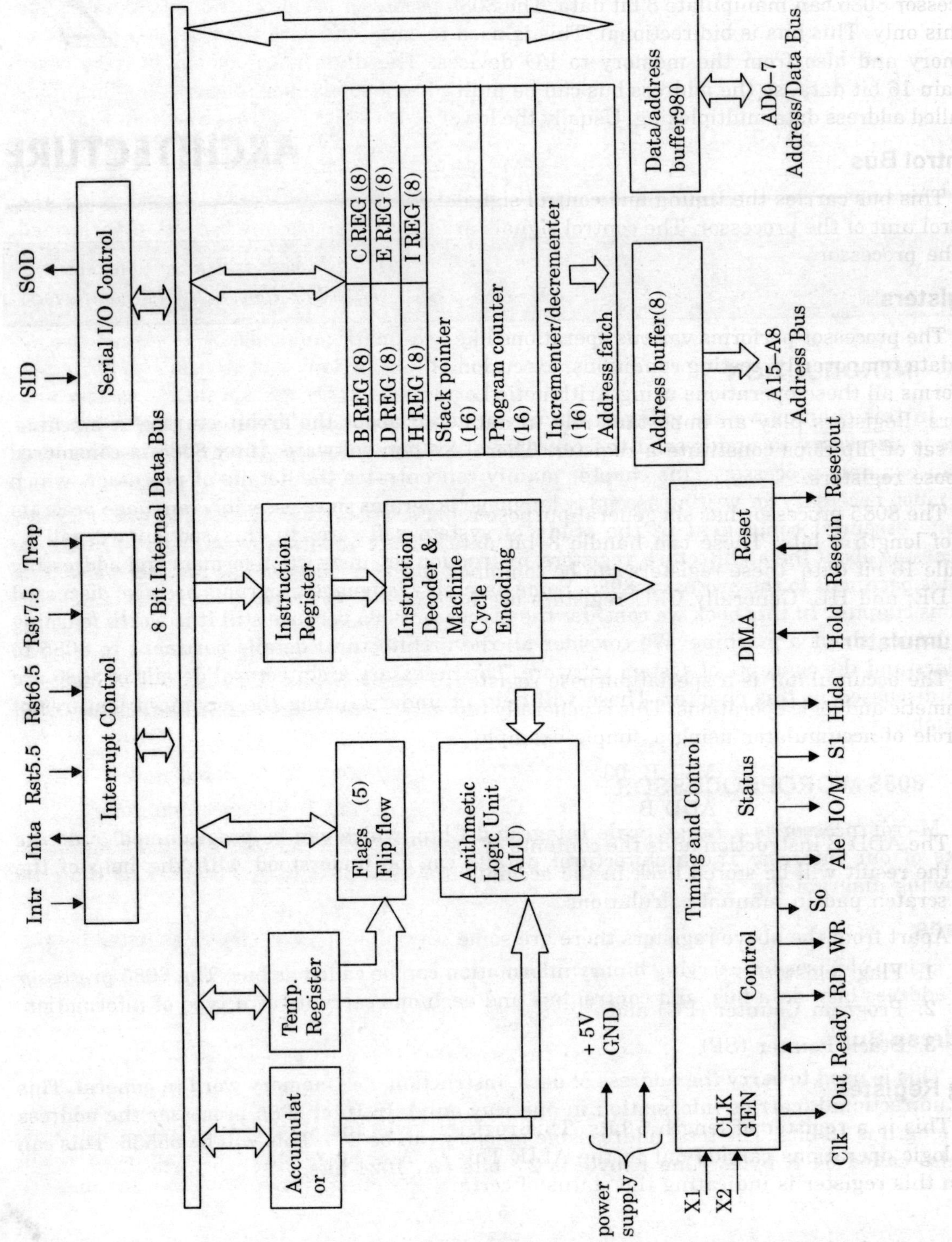

Fig. 2.1 Architecture of 8085 microprocessor

Data Bus

This bus is used to carry the data. This carries the memory word. The length is 8 bits. This can be also called the word length of the processor. We can understand that the processor 8085 can manipulate 8 bit data. The 8085 processor is called as 8 bit processor due to this only. This bus is bidirectional. This is used to carry the data from the I/O devices to memory and also from the memory to I/O devices. The data bus may not be able carry certain 16 bit data, so the address bus can be multiplexed sometimes to carry the data. This is called address data multiplexing. Usually the lower order 8 bit of address bus is multiplexed.

Control Bus

This bus carries the timing and control signals, which are generated by the timing and control unit of the processor. The control signals are used to enable any operation performed by the processor.

Registers

The processor performs various operations like arithmetic and logical operations, storing the data temporarily, testing conditions, execution of instructions and others. The processor performs all these operations using Arithmetic Logic Unit (ALU), control unit, registers and others. Registers play an important role in data manipulation. These are programmable. The set of flip-flops constitute a register. There are general-purpose registers and special purpose registers.

The 8085 processor has six general-purpose registers namely B, C, D, E, H and L. These are of length 8 bits. These can handle 8–bit data during program execution. In order to handle 16 bit data, these registers can be combined together and used as register pairs like BC, DE, and HL. Generally CPU registers are high speed registers.

Accumulator

The accumulator is a special purpose register of length 8–bits. This is used to perform arithmetic and logic operations. This is generally represented as register A. We can understand the role of accumulator using a simple example.

```
MVI B, 03        // Move 03 to B register
ADD B            // Add B with accumulator
```

The ADD B instruction adds the contents of register B with the contents of accumulator and the result will be stored back in the accumulator only. This is exactly playing the role of a scratch pad in manual calculations.

Apart from the above registers there are some special purpose registers as listed below:

1. Flag register
2. Program Counter (PC) and
3. Stack Pointer (SP)

Flag Register

This is a register of length 5 bits. This register gives the status of various arithmetic and logic operations carried out in the ALU. This is used for testing the conditions. Each bit in this register is indicating the status of certain operation. These are given hereunder.

CARRY (CY) — It is set to '1', if operation results a carry, otherwise '0' is set.

ZERO (Z) — It is set to '1', if result of an operation is zero, otherwise 0 is set.

SIGN (S) — It is set to '1' for negative numbers and 0 for unsigned numbers.

Parity (P) — It is set to depending on the number of ones and zeros depends On which type of parity is used (Odd or Even parity).

Auxiliary Carry (AC) — It is based on the result of a computation at an intermediate stage.

Program Counter (PC)

It is special purpose register used as a pointer to the machine instructions to be executed. It will have the address of next instruction to be executed. It is 16 bit register since it is used to the address of the instruction.

Stack Pointer (SP)

It is also special purpose register used as a pointer to memory used in subroutines and other logical division of programs. It is of length 16 bit since it is pointing a memory location.

Data Formats

There are different data formats available to represent the data for the computer use. Some examples are:

ASCII code format

BCD code format

ASCII code: It is actually acronym of **A**merican **S**tandard **C**ode for **I**nformation **I**nterchange. This format widely used. It is actually code to represent the information of length 7 bits. In this code each character is assigned a hexadecimal equivalent, which is understandable for the processor. The ASCII equivalent of the character a is 61 and for A it is 41. Similarly for all the symbols and numbers there are ASCII equivalent hexadecimal codes are available. This is one type of data format used for representing the information understandable by processor.

BCD code: It is acronym of **B**inary **C**oded **D**ecimal. This is data format for representing decimal numbers. The decimal numbers 0 to 9 can be represented in BCD from 0000 to 1001. This code can represent only the decimal numbers.

2.3 INSTRUCTION SET

The set of instructions available for a processor is called as the instruction set of that processor. It is completely dependent on the architecture of the processor. It will vary processor to processor. Using these instructions we will be able to write assembly language program. Group of such instructions will constitute an assembly language program. The assembly language programs are discussed in detail in later sections of this chapter. There are some examples for instructions from different categories are discussed hereunder. Different types of instructions are listed below. Only few examples are discussed for each category of instructions.

1. Data transfer instructions
2. Arithmetic and logic instructions
3. Loop instructions
4. Machine control instructions
5. Flag manipulation instructions
6. Shift and rotate instructions and
7. Others

Data Transfer Instructions

This type of instructions is used for transferring the data from one register to another register, one memory location to register and vice versa. The data can also be directly transferred to the register. Few examples are given below:

MOV B, A

The contents are transferred from the source register A (accumulator) to the destination register B. Here actually the data are copied from the source register A to the destination register B. The result of this execution will allow the register A and B to have the same contents *i.e.*, the content of A. Actually this type of instructions can be considered as data copy instructions.

MVI B, 04

In this case the hexadecimal data 04 will be transferred the register B. This directly transfers data to the register.

Arithmetic and Logic Instructions

This type of instructions is used to perform arithmetic and logical operations. Some examples are listed below:

SUB B

The SUB B instruction subtracts the contents of register B from the contents of accumulator and the result stores back the result in the accumulator.

ORA B

This instruction performs logical OR with the contents of register B.

Similarly the other groups of instructions will perform the corresponding operations. The reader can find many examples for these groups in some other microprocessor books. The purpose of introducing the architectural features in this chapter is to give the readers a basis for understanding the system software concepts. The architectural details, which are directly or indirectly help in understanding the system software concepts, are only discussed in this chapter.

Instruction Format

It specifies how the opcode and operand (data) and other control information are present in an instruction. This format depends on the length of the instruction. There are some examples given below for the instructions in 8085.

In a broad sense the instruction formats can be grouped as mentioned below:

1. One byte instructions
2. Two byte instructions and
3. Three byte instructions

This classification is based on the length of the instructions. If the instruction length is one then such type of instructions is grouped the first category. The format will also be of length one byte. For example,

SUB B

The SUB B instruction subtracts the contents of register B from the contents of accumulator and stores the result back in the accumulator. The opcode in this instruction is SUB and the operand is B. The corresponding Hex code for this instruction is 90. The binary equivalent of this 90 in a single byte addressable machine is '1001 0000'. This occupies only one byte.

ADI 04

The ADI instruction adds the data specified in the instruction itself 04 to the contents of accumulator and stores the result back in the accumulator. The opcode in this instruction is SUB and the operand is B. The corresponding Hex code for this instruction is C6. The binary equivalent of this C6 is '1100 0011'. This occupies one byte and the data 04 (0000 0100) occupies one byte. Totally this instruction occupies two bytes.

STA 8900

This instruction stores the contents of the accumulator (result) in the location 8900. The opcode in this instruction is STA and the address for storing the operand is specified in the instruction. The corresponding Hex code for this instruction is 32. The binary equivalent of this 32 is '0011 0010'. This occupies one byte and the address 89 00 occupies two bytes. Totally this instruction occupies three bytes.

32	0011 0010
89	1000 1001
00	0000 0000

Note: Opcode is the acronym of **Op**eration **Code** to be performed. It is in hexadecimal code.

2.4 ADDRESSING MODES

This is a format for specifying the operands (data) in an instruction. There are different types of addressing modes available. Few types are listed below:

1. Immediate addressing
2. Direct addressing
3. Register addressing and
4. Indirect addressing

Immediate Addressing

In this group the operand is (data) explicitly specified in the instruction itself. The data is immediately available. This is part of the instruction itself. For exmaple,

ADI 04

The data 04 is immediately available.

Direct Addressing

In direct addressing mode the memory address is directly specified in the instruction itself. The operand is available in the address specified. For example,

LXI H, 8800

This instruction loads the address 8800 into the HL register pair.

The operand is available in the location 8800. The instruction has the address directly as one of its component.

Register Addressing

In this addressing mode the operand is available in a register and it can only be used by another register. The operands can only be specified and used only by the registers. For example,

MOV B, A

The contents are transferred from the source register A (accumulator) to the destination register B. Here only the registers refer the operands.

Indirect Addressing

In this addressing mode the address of the operand is indirectly specified. For example,

MOV B, M

The contents of the memory location have the address of the operand to be used. M stands for Memory, and its value depends on previous instruction.

2.5 ASSEMBLY LANGUAGE PROGRAMS

Assembly language program is a program written using mnemonics present in a processor. Mnemonics are like symbols. These are actually memory aids (for the programmers). These are acronyms of some operations. These are abbreviated names of binary instructions. For example,

'ADD' is mnemonics for addition operation

'SUB' is mnemonics for subtraction operation

We will write a simple assembly language program using the instruction set of the 8085 processor. This example follows the mnemonics and opcode of 8085 instruction set.

Address	**Mnemonics**	**Comments**
8800	SUB A	//Clear the accumulator
8801	MVI A, 02	// Move 02 to accumulator
8803	MVI B, 03	// Move 03 to B register
8805	ADD B	// Add B with accumulator
8806	STA 8900	//store the result in 8900
8807	HLT	// Halt the execution

Fig. 2.2 A simple assembly language program for adding two numbers

Similarly we can write many assembly language programs using the instruction set of the processor.

2.6 ARCHITECTURAL FEATURES OF 8086

In this section we will see some important features of 8086. This will help understanding the advanced concepts in system programming especially in assemblers and loaders.

This processor is a 16-bit processor. The data bus length is 16 bits. It has a powerful instruction set which exploits the advanced architectural features of 8086. Z8000 is the 16-bit processor by Zilog. MC 68000 is the 16 bit processor by Motorola.

The 8086 processor has two independent functional units, which are given below:

1. Bus Interface Unit (BIU)
2. Execution Unit (EU)

2.7 BUS INTERFACE UNIT (BIU)

Bus Interface Unit is responsible for transfer of instructions, addresses and data on the system bus to the execution unit. It handles the transfer of data between the processor, memory and I/O devices. It includes instruction fetch, data fetch, address transfer and computation of effective address of the memory. Instruction Queue (IQ), segment registers and Instruction Pointers (IP) are the functional units of the Bus Interface Unit.

Instruction Queue (IQ)

Instruction queue keeps the instructions ready for execution. It is six bytes in length. It can keep six instructions bytes, which can be fetched in advance from the memory. This speeds up the execution. The Instruction queue can fetch one instruction while the execution unit executes another instruction. The bus interface unit and the execution unit can work simultaneously while the execution unit does not use the system bus. This leads to **pipelining.** The process of fetching one instruction in advance from the memory (to be executed next), while the execution unit is executing another instruction is called pipelining.

Segment Registers

The 8086 processor has data bus length as 16 bits, and the address bus length is 20 bits. The addressable memory is $2^{20} = 1$ MB. This memory is divided into 16 logical segments. Each segment is containing 64 k bytes of memory. There are four segment registers in 8086 processor. They are

1. Code Segment Register (CS)
2. Data Segment Register (DS)
3. Extra Segment Register (ES)
4. Stack Segment Register (SS)

The code segment is used to store the code (the program to be executed). The data segment stores the data, which is necessary for execution. The extra segment also stores the data, which can be sometimes treated as another data segment. The stack segment is used to store the stack data. The CPU generally uses the stack as a temporary storage. The CS, DS, ES and SS segment registers are used for addressing the respective segments. They contain the segment addresses for respective segments. These registers store the 16 bit starting address for the four memory segments. The Bus Interface Unit generates 20 bit starting address using the segment and the offset components of an address. This BIU can address from 0000 to FFFFF. These are the base addresses of the respective segments.

Instruction Pointer (IP)

This can also be called as the program counter. It holds the address of the next instruction to be executed. The physical address can be computed using the base addresses in the segment registers and offsets in the pointers and index registers. The 20 bit address can be calculated using the two 16 bit addresses. The base address is shifted four bits left and added with the offset.

2.8 EXECUTION UNIT

The other important functional part of 8086 is execution unit. This is responsible for execution of any instruction. The functional parts of the execution unit are given below:

1. Control unit and instruction decoder
2. Arithmetic and Logic Unit (ALU)
3. Flag register
4. General purpose registers
5. Stack pointer register
6. Pointer and index register

Control Unit and Instruction Decoder

It generates the necessary control and timing signals for all operations of the processor. The instruction decoding for execution is performed in the instruction decoder. The execution of an instruction involves the following steps.

1. Fetching
2. Decoding
3. Executing.

Arithmetic and Logic Unit (ALU)

This performs 8 or 16 bit arithmetic operations such as addition, subtraction, multiplication, division, data conversion and also the logical operations like NOT, OR, and AND. It also performs register increment, decrement and shift operations.

Flag Registers

As in 8085, the 8086 flag register indicates the results of computations in the ALU. It does similar functions of 8085 flag register. It stores the information about the status of the processor and the status of the instruction executed. The 8086 processor has nine single bit flags to reflect the status of the CPU. The flag register can only be handled using the processor control instructions such as CLC (CLear Carry), CMC (CoMplement Carry), STC (SeT Carry), CLD (CLear Direction Flag) and arithmetic instructions. Each bit in this register is indicating the status of certain operation. These are given hereunder.

CARRY (CY) — It is set to '1', if operation results a carry, otherwise '0' is set.

ZERO (Z) — It is set to '1', if result of an operation is zero, otherwise 0 is set.

SIGN (S) — It is set to '1' for negative numbers and 0 for unsigned numbers.

Parity (P) — If the lower order bits of the result contains the even number of 1s then it is set to '1'.

Auxiliary Carry (AC) — It is based on the result of a computation at an intermediate stage.

Trap Flag — This is set to '1' during Interrupt (Trap)

Direction Flag—this is used while a string is processed. It is set to '1' if the string is processed from the higher address to lower address. It is set to '0' if the string is processed from the lower address to higher address. The index pointers are incremented or decremented based on the DF status.

Overflow Flag—this is set to '1' if an addition produces a carry out of MSB. If the subtraction produces borrow, then also it set to '1'. Such case, it is called as under flow.

General Purpose Registers

The 8066 processor has general purpose and special purpose registers of length 16 bits. The general purpose registers are used for holding the data, intermediate result and the like. The special purpose registers are used as segment registers, pointers, index registers or as offset storage registers for particular addressing modes. The general-purpose registers are AX, BX, CX and DX. The register AX can be used as the accumulator. This can be used as a combination of AL and AH. The AL is used for lower 8 bits and AH is used for higher 8 bits. This is possible for all the general purpose registers of 8086. It is because that this processor is to be compatible with the Intel 8085 processor. X is used to represent the 16 bit register. The BX register functions as base register. It is used as pointer also. The CX register can be used as a count register. The DX register can be used as an I/O address pointer in the IN and OUT instructions. This is effectively used in data movements and in the case of arithmetic and logic instructions execution.

Pointers and Index Registers

The Intel 8086 processor has pointers and index registers. The pointers are

1. Instruction Pointer (IP)
2. Base Pointer (BP)
3. Stack Pointer (SP)

The index registers are

1. Source Index (SI)
2. Destination Index (DI)

The pointers keep the offset for the segments. The instruction pointers keeps the offset for code segment. The BP and SP keep the offsets for data and stack segments respectively.

The index registers also keep the offsets. They are also sometimes used as general purpose registers. The SI is used to store the offset of source data in data segment. The DI is used to store the offset of destination in data segment.

2.9 ADDRESSING MODES

We have already seen some addressing modes in case of the 8085 processor. Addressing mode can be defined as a method of specifying the effective address of the operands in the memory. There are nine addressing modes in the 8086 processor. They are listed below:

1. Immediate addressing mode
2. Implicit addressing mode
3. Direct addressing mode
4. Indirect addressing mode
5. Register addressing mode
6. Register indirect addressing mode
7. Based indexed addressing mode
8. Register relative addressing mode and
9. Relative based indexed addressing mode

We will see about each addressing mode in brief in this section.

Immediate Addressing Mode

In this addressing mode data are immediately available. The data will be part of the instruction itself.

For example, MOV AX, 200; Move the datum 200 to the accumulator.

Implicit Addressing Mode

The instruction assumes that the data implicitly. The data will be implicitly specified in registers in this addressing mode. These are also called zero address instructions.

CMC; this is processor control instruction. This is to CoMplement the Carry, which is implicitly available.

Direct addressing Mode

In this addressing mode address of the operand is part of the instruction itself.

MOV AX, [4000H]; here the contents of the address 4000 will be moved to the register AX.

Indirect Addressing Mode

In this addressing mode the address of the operand is indirectly specified in a register. The address of the operand will be available in a register.

MOV AX, [BX]; The register BX will keep the address of the operand. The operand specified by the address will be transferred to the register AX.

Register Addressing Mode

In this addressing mode the operands are specified in the registers. The registers are used for addressing the operands.

ADD AX, BX; the contents of BX are added with AX and the result is stored in the register AX.

Register Indirect Addressing Mode

In this addressing mode the effective address of the operand is specified in the base register (BX) or in the index registers (SI and DI), which are specified in the instruction.

MOV AX, [BX];

The operand is specified by the address specified by the base register.

Based Indexed Addressing Mode

In this addressing mode, the effective address is generated by adding the contents of the base register (BX or BP), to the contents of the index register (SI or DI).

MOV AX, [BX] [SI]; the contents of BX and SI are added to give address of the operand.

Register Relative Addressing Mode

In this addressing mode adding the contents of any of the base registers (BX or BP) or index registers (SI or DI) with the 8 bit or 16 bit displacement value, generates the effective address.

MOV AX, 40H [BX]; the displacement value is 40H. This is added with the contents of the base register to produce the effective address.

Relative Based Indexed Addressing Mode

In this addressing mode the effective address is produced by adding the contents of base register (BX or BP) with the contents of index register (SI or DI) and the 8 bit or 16 bit displacement value.

MOV AX, 40H [BX] [SI]; the displacement value 40H is added with the contents of BX and SI to produce the effective address.

2.10 INSTRUCTION SET OF 8086

The 8086 instructions are classified into the following groups:

1. Data transfer instructions
2. Arithmetic instructions
3. Bit manipulation instructions
4. String instructions
5. Control instructions and
6. Processor control instructions

We will see about these instruction groups with few examples. In this section we are discussing the instructions in very brief manner only. This is to give an idea about the instructions in the 8086 processor.

Data Transfer Instructions

These instructions are responsible for the data transfer from the source operand to destination operand. The way in which they transfer data depends on the addressing mode. All the store, move, load, exchange, input and output instructions are coming under this category. We will see some examples.

Examples for data transfer instructions:

1. MOV destination, source; MOV AX, BX

Here the data are transferred from register or memory or immediate operand to register or memory.

2. XCHG destination, source; XCHG [4000H], AX

Here exchange of contents from source to destination and vice versa is done.

3. IN accumulator, port or DX; IN AL, 0440H

This instruction reads data from 8 bit port whose address is specified and stores in the AL register or reads data from 16 bit port whose address is specified in DX and stores in the AL register.

4. OUT port or DX accumulator; OUT 0400H, AL

This instruction writes the data available in AL to a 8 bit port whose address is specified or writes data available in AX to a 16 bit port whose address is specified in DX.

5. XLAT

These type instructions are translation instructions, which are used for converting the codes in case of code conversion problems.

Arithmetic Logic Instructions

All the instructions performing arithmetic, logical, increment, decrement, compare and scan operations are coming under this category. We will see some examples in this group.

1. ADD destination, source; ADD AX, BX

The contents of source and destination are added and the result is stored in the destination itself.

2. ADC destination, source; ADD AX, BX

The contents of source and destination are added along with the carry and the result is stored in the destination.

3. INC destination; INC AX

This instruction adds 1 to contents of the destination specified in the instruction.

4. DEC destination; DEC AX

This instruction subtracts 1 from the contents of the destination specified in the instruction.

5. AND destination, source; ADD AX, BX

This instruction performs logical AND operation between source and destination.

Bit Manipulation Instructions

These instructions perform the bit wise operations like shifting or rotating in either direction with or without count in CX.

1. SHL destination, count;

This instruction performs the left shifting of the destination operand by the number of counts specified in the count value.

2. SHR destination, count;

This instruction performs the right shifting of the destination operand by the number of counts specified in the count value.

3. ROL destination, count;

This instruction performs the left rotating of the destination operand by the number of counts specified in the count value.

String Instructions

These instructions involve various string manipulation operations like move, load, scan, compare and others.

MOV S;

This instruction moves the string to the AL/AX register.

REP;

This instruction used to repeat the string operations until the count value becomes zero, which is available in the CX register.

SCAS;

This instruction performs the scanning of the string, which is specified in the AL or AX register.

Control Instructions

These instructions transfer the control of execution to some specified address. All types of conditional, unconditional branch instructions, jump, interrupt and return instructions will be falling under this category. The instructions, which cause loops, are also coming under this category.

JUMP target; JUMP 4000H

This instruction causes transfer of control to the address 4000H unconditionally. This is an unconditional branch instruction.

LOOP target; LOOP label;

This instruction executes a loop from the address specified or from label, until the value in CX register value becomes zero.

RET;

This instruction returns the control at the end of procedure.

Processor Control Instructions

These instructions control the processor. These are also called as machine control instructions. NOP, HLT and WAIT are some examples for machine control instructions.

NOP;

This instruction puts the machine in idle state *i.e.*, the processor does no operation.

WAIT;

This instruction puts the machine in wait state.

HLT;

This instruction halts the processor.

2.11 ASSEMBLY LANGUAGE PROGRAMS IN 8086

As we have seen in the case of the Intel 8085 processor, here also we will see some examples for assembly language programs based on 8086 instruction set. This will not discuss the all the details of writing assembly language programs. This is to give an introduction to assembly language programs in the 8086 instruction set.

Example 2.1

The following program is to add two numbers, which stored in the data segment at two different offsets. The data segment is initialized with 3000H. The result is stored at another offset from the initial address.

```
MOV AX, 3000H        ] —
MOV DS, AX           ] — Initialize the Data segment with the value 3000H.
MOV AX, [0400H]        — Move the contents from the address using the offset 400H
                         to AX register.
ADD AX, [0500H]        — Add the contents of AX with the operand specified in the
                         offset 500H.
MOV [0700H], AX        — Store the result in the offset 0700H.
HLT                    — Stop the execution.
```

Example 2.2

```
          ASSUME CS: CODE, DS: DATA
          CODE SEGMENT
          ORG 200H
START:    LEA BX, 1500H
          MOV CX, 50D
LABEL:    MOV [BX], 00
          INC BX
          LOOP LABEL
          HLT
CODE      ENDS
          END
```

This program uses the code segment and data segment. This is to clear 50 consecutive bytes from the memory starting from 1500 onwards. This starting address is stored in BX register. This uses LOOP also. Each time the BX registers is incremented and '00' is moved to clear the memory location.

2.12 EXAMPLE ARCHITECTURES

In this section we will be seeing some examples for different architectures. Only the salient features are addressed.

2.12.1 Intel 80286

The Intel 80286 is a high performance 16 bit microprocessor. It has been designed for multi user and multi tasking system. It has memory management capability, four level memory protection features. It supports virtual memory. It can directly address up to 16M bytes of physical memory. It can manage 1 GB of virtual memory. The clock frequency varies from 8MHz to 12.5MHz. It has 24 address lines and 16 data lines. It uses mathematical coprocessors. The concepts of registers, instructions, and addressing modes are very similar to 8086 architecture. This processor operates either in real address mode or protected virtual address mode. In the real address mode it can address up to 1MB of physical memory. The virtual address mode is for multi user and multi tasking operating system. This mode is protected mode.

The 80286 contains four processing units. They are listed below:

1. Bus unit
2. Instruction unit
3. Execution unit and
4. Address unit

The bus unit performs all the memory and I/O operations. It can pre fetch the instructions and store in queue. The Instruction Unit decodes the pre fetched instructions and keeps it in a queue for execution. The execution unit executes the instructions. The Address Unit computes the addresses of memory or I/O devices for read and write operations. All the units can work in a pipelined fashion. This processor has pipelining feature. In pipelining several works can be executed simultaneously by the single processor.

2.12.2 Intel 80386

It is a 32-bit microprocessor. It is compatible with other 16 bit processors also. It has a separate Memory Management Unit (MMU) on the chip. It has four level protection mechanisms. The data bus length is 32 bits. It has 32 non-multiplexed address buses. It can address up to 4GB of memory. The virtual memory capacity offered by the MMU is 64 Tera Bytes (64 X10^{12}). The clock frequencies are 25, 33, 40 MHz. The page size is 4 KB and the segments vary in size. (Segmentation and paging are operating system concepts. These are addressed in the operating system chapter (chapter no. 3)).

The 80386 is highly pipelined. It has six functional units. The additional two units from 80286 are segmentation unit and page unit. It supports paging and segmentation. It supports 11 addressing modes. This processor has eight 32-bit general purpose registers, six 16-bit segment registers, one 32-bit instruction pointer, six debug registers and a 32-bit status register. The 80386 has a segment descriptor register associated with each segment register.

2.12.3 Intel 80486

Intel 80486 is a 32 bit processor. It has a 32 bit CPU, a floating point math co processor, unified instruction and data cache memory and memory management unit in a single IC. The clock various clock frequencies available are 25, 33, 66 and 100 MHz. It can directly address up to 4GB memory. The memory management unit provides 64 TB virtual memory. The address bus length is 24 bits. The data bus length is 32 bits. It has 11 addressing modes.

The 80486 processor has the following functional units:

1. Execution unit
2. Control unit
3. Bus interface unit
4. Code pre fetch unit
5. Instruction decode unit

6. Segmentation unit
7. Cache unit and
8. Floating point unit

All the units are responsible for the respective operations. The Execution unit, Control unit, Bus Interface Units are all doing the conventional functions. The code pre fetch unit also contains a 32 bit queue to store fetched instruction codes. The control unit has additional control memory to store the micro code. The segmentation unit converts the logical address into physical address. It provides four level protection for protecting operating system and user programs. The page unit provides paging within the segment.

2.12.4 Instruction Types

The 80 × 86 (80286, 80386, 80486) instruction set is composed of six main groups of instructions. The instructions of Intel based architectures are given hereunder. These will give some idea about the architectural differences of various 80 × 86 architectures.

Data Transfer Instructions

The data transfer instructions are:

IN	Input byte or word from port
LAHF	Load AH from Flags
LDS	Load pointer using data Segment
LEA	Load Effective Address
LES	Load pointer using Extra Segment
MOV	MOVe to/from register/memory
OUT	OUTput byte or word to port
POP	POP word off stack
POPF	POP Flags off stack
PUSH	PUSH word into stack
PUSHF	PUSH Flags into stack
SAHF	Store AH into Flags
XCHG	Exchange byte or word
XLAT	Translate byte

Additional 80286 instructions are:

INS	INput String from port
OUTS	OUTput String to port
POPA	POP All registers
PUSHA	PUSH All registers

Additional 80386 instructions are:

LFS	Load pointer using FS
LGS	Load pointer using GS

LSS	Load pointer using SS
MOVSX	MOVe with Sign eXtended
MOVZX	MOVe with Zero eXtended
POPAD	POP All Double (32-bit) registers
POPD	POP Double register
POPFD	POP Double Flag register
PUSHAD	PUSH All Double registers
PUSHD	PUSH Double register
PUSHFD	PUSH Double Flag register

Additional 80486 instruction is:

BSWAP	Byte SWAP

New Pentium instruction is:

MOV	Move to/from control register

Arithmetic Instructions

The arithmetic instructions are:

AAA	ASCII adjust for addition
AAD	ASCII adjust for division
AAM	ASCII adjust for multiply
AAS	ASCII adjust for subtraction
ADC	Add byte or word plus carry
ADD	Add byte or word
CBW	Convert byte or word
CMP	Compare byte or word
CWD	Convert word or double word
DAA	Decimal adjust for addition
DAS	Decimal adjust for subtraction
DEC	Decrement byte or word by one
DIV	Divide byte or word (unsigned)
IDI	Integer divide byte or word
IMUL	Integer multiply byte or word
INC	Increment byte or word by one
MUL	Multiply byte or word (unsigned)
NEG	Negate byte or word
SBB	Subtract byte or word and carry
SUB	Subtract byte or word

Additional 80386 instructions are:

CDQ	Convert double word to quad word

CWDE	Convert word to double word

Additional 80486 instructions are:

CMPXCHG	Compare and exchange
XADD	Exchange and add

New Pentium instruction is:

CMPXCHG8B	Compare and exchange 8 bytes

Bit Manipulation Instructions

The bit manipulation instructions are:

AND	Logical AND of byte or word
NOT	Logical NOT of byte or word
OR	Logical OR of byte or word
RCL	Rotate left through carry byte or word
RCR	Rotate right through carry byte or word
ROL	Rotate left byte or word
ROR	Rotate right byte or word
SAL	Arithmetic shift left byte or word
SAR	Arithmetic shift right byte or word
SHL	Logical shift left byte or word
SHR	Logical shift right byte or word
TEST	Test byte or word
XOR	Logical exclusive-OR of byte or word

Additional 80386 instructions are:

BSF	Bit scan forward
BSR	Bit scan reverse
BT	Bit test
BTC	Bit test and complement
BTR	Bit test and reset
BTS	Bit test and set
SETcc	Set byte on condition
SHLD	Shift left double precision
SHRD	Shift right double precision

String Instructions

The string instructions are:

CMPS	Compare byte or word string
LODS	Load byte or word string

MOVS	Move byte or word string
MOVSB (MOVSW)	Move byte string(word string)
REP	Repeat
REPE (REPZ)	Repeat while equal (zero)
REPNE (REPNZ)	Repeat while not equal (not zero)
SCAS	Scan byte or word string
STOS	Store byte or word string

Program Transfer Instructions

The program transfer instructions are:

CALL	Call procedure (subroutine)
INT	Interrupt
INTO	Interrupt if overflow
IRET	Return from interrupt
JA (JNBE)	Jump if above (not below or equal)
JAE (JNB)	Jump if above or equal (not below)
JB (JNAE)	Jump if below (not above or equal)
JBE (JNA)	Jump if below or equal (not above)
JC	Jump if carry set
JCXZ	Jump if CX equals zero
JE (JZ)	Jump if equal (zero)
JG (JNLE)	Jump if greater (not less or equal)
JGE (JNL)	Jump if greater or equal (not less)
JL (JNGE)	Jump if less (not greater or equal)
JLE (JNG)	Jump if less or equal (not greater)
JMP	Unconditional jump
JNC	Jump if no carry
JNE (JNZ)	Jump if not equal (not zero)
JNO	Jump if no overflow
JNP (JPO)	Jump if no parity (parity odd)
JNS	Jump if no sign
JO	Jump if overflow
JP (JPE)	Jump if parity (parity even)
JS	Jump if sign
LOOP	Loop unconditional
LOOPE (LOOPZ)	Loop if equal (zero)
LOOPNE (LOOPNZ)	Loop if not equal (not zero)

RET	Return from procedure (subroutine)

Additional 80286 instructions are:

BOUND	Check index against array bounds
ENTER	Enter a procedure
LEAVE	Leave a procedure

Additional 80386 instructions are:

IRETD	Interrupt return
JECXZ	Jump if ECX is zero

Processor Control Instructions

The processor control instructions are:

CLC	Clear carry flag
CLD	Clear direction flag
CLI	Clear interrupt enable flag
CMC	Complement carry flag
ESC	Escape to external processor
HLT	Halt processor
LOCK	Lock bus during next instruction
NOP	No operation
STC	Set carry flag
STD	Set direction flag
STI	Set interrupt enable flag
WAIT	Wait for TEST pin activity

Additional 80286 instructions (protected mode only) are:

ARPL	Adjust requested privilege level
CLTS	Clear task switched flag
LAR	Load access rights
LGDT	Load global descriptor table
LIDT	Load interrupt descriptor table
LLDT	Load local descriptor table
LMSW	Load machine status word
LSL	Load segment limit
LTR	Load task register
SGDT	Store global descriptor table
SIDT	Store interrupt descriptor table
SLDT	Store local descriptor table
SMSW	Store machine status word

STR	Store task register
VERR	Verify segment for reading
VE	Verify segment for writing

Additional 80486 instructions are:

INVD	Invalidate cache
INVLPG	Invalidate TLB entry
WBINVD	Write back and invalidate cache

New pentium instructions are:

CPUID	CPU identification
RDMSR	Read from model-specific register
RDTSC	Read from timestamp counter
RSM	Resume from system management mode
WRMSR	Write to model-specific register

The instructions listed for the architectures 80286, 80386, 80486 and Pentium will give the idea about the architectural details of those processors. Some of the instructions will be now and then used in this book. All these architectures are Intel based architectures only.

Summary

In this chapter we have seen the architecture, instruction set, addressing modes, assembly language programs of Intel 8085, 8086 processors. These fundamental concepts of these processors are dealt in detail. These concepts are very much necessary for learning the concepts related system software. Unless these concepts are understood the readers will not able to understand the concepts of the system software. This chapter discusses the architecture and other details in brief manner only. The readers are further advised to refer some books on microprocessors for more details if necessary.

QUESTIONS

Part A

1. Name few types of hypothetical computer model.
2. What is known as instruction set?
3. What are the addressing modes?
4. What are the types of instruction formats in Intel 8085?
5. What are the salient features of 8086 Architecture?
6. What are the addressing modes used in 8085 and 8086?
7. What is immediate addressing?
8. What is the use of program counter?
9. What are types of instructions in Intel architectures?
10. Write few assembly language program based in the 8085 instruction set.
11. Write few assembly language program based in the 8086 instruction set.

12. Compare the 8085 and 8086 based on the registers.

13. What the segments available in 8086 and write note briefly?

14. What is a control register?

15. What is the data bus?

Part B

1. Write in detail about Intel 8085 Architecture.

2. Write about the functions of Intel 8085.

3. Explain the architectural details of 8086 machine.

4. What is the relationship between the system software and the machine structure? (Assume any architecture).

5. Compare 8085 and 8086 architectures.

6. Write in detail about addressing modes available in 8085 with examples.

7. Write in detail about addressing modes available in 8086 with examples.

8. What are the instruction formats available in 8085 and 8086 and explain?

9. How does an instruction set affect the assembly language program development? Explain with examples.

10. Compare the instruction set of 8085 and 8086 architectures.

11. Write note on the following processors:

(*i*) Intel 80286 architecture

(*ii*) Intel 80386 architecture

(*iii*) Intel 80486 architecture

CHAPTER 3

OPERATING SYSTEM

Blessed are the meek,
For they shall inherit the earth.

3.1 INTRODUCTION

This chapter discusses about the fundamentals of operating systems and other concepts in detail. Mainly process management, memory management of operating system are given more attention because these are associated with the system software. In fact whole of this book is written around the chapters compilers and operating systems. At the end of this chapter the reader will be familiar with the concepts of operating system, which are pertinent to the system software.

3.2 OPERATING SYSTEM

The operating system is a system program. In the first chapter (Introduction to system software), we have discussed a simple analogy between the wild animal and computer. In which we have seen that the controlling element is the system software. If we say the **controlling element** is operating system then it will be more appropriate. That analogy is more appropriate to the operating system. Some of the definitions about the operating system are listed below:

1. The operating system is the controlling element for the computer. It is a control program, which controls the execution of user programs.
2. The operating system is an environment, which allows the user to communicate and control the computer.
3. The operating system is a program, which acts as an intermediary between the user and the computer.

The government does not do any useful functions. But it allows many useful functions to be carried out by providing support. We can understand this way also *i.e.*, the government creates an environment in which the useful functions can be carried out. In a similar way the operating system also creates an environment in which the useful functions can be carried out. *The operating system creates easy and convenient environment for the users* in order to carry out useful operations.

The computer has many resources like CPU, memory, I/O devices, software and others. The operating system is like a manager of theses resources of the machine. It allocates these resources to programs and users. We can also say that the operating system is a resource allocator.

From the above discussions we can understand that the operating system is an intermediary between the user and computer. It is a control program and resource allocator. Apart from these it is a system program, which also coordinates other system programs.

In a computer system processor, main memory, secondary memory and other peripherals are available. We will see how the operating system is organized among these entities. This can be easily understood by the following Fig. 3.1.

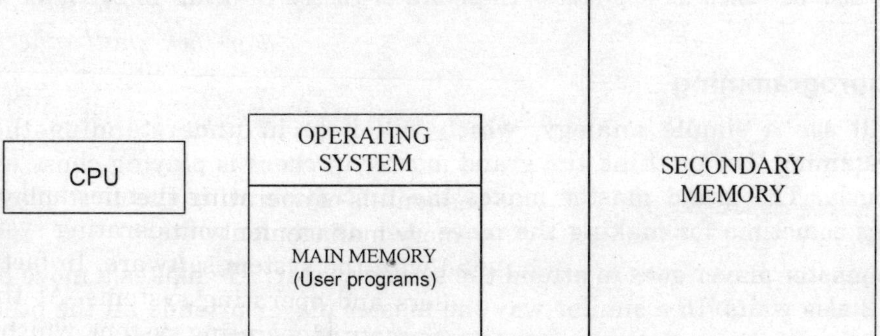

Fig. 3.1 Organization of operating system in a computer system

The CPU does the arithmetic and logical calculations. In the main memory only, the execution is taking place. This memory is actually volatile in nature. The operating system is placed in this memory only. The remaining space in the main memory can be allotted for the user programs. The size of this main memory is small.

The secondary memory is auxiliary storage device. It is non-volatile in nature. All the data can be permanently stored in this secondary memory. The required data can be brought into the main memory from the secondary memory. Similarly the data can be brought out from main memory to the secondary memory. *The method of bringing in the data from secondary memory to main memory is called as swap in. The method of bringing out the data from the main memory to secondary memory is called swap out.* The size of this type of memory is large. The secondary memory is also called back store.

3.3 OPERATING SYSTEM TECHNIQUES AND TYPES

In the subsequent section we are going to see some important operating system techniques like batch processing, multi programming, time-sharing and others. We can also say that these are operating system types. These are actually evolutions of operating system aiming to improve the performance *i.e.*, computer utilization.

The early operating system was called as Simple Monitor. It was consuming large time. The performance was very poor. Large amount of time was wasted in loading and unloading the compiler for the different programs written in various programming languages.

3.3.1 Batch Processing

Grouping similar jobs together is called Batch processing. The similar jobs refer to the jobs written in a particular programming language. This is one type operating system technique. This will increase the computer utilization. This actually reduces the set up time for the jobs. This avoids frequent loading and unloading of compilers and other necessary system software. In this case the operating system was called as **Batch Monitor**. There was slight improvement in the performance.

Note: The term job refers to a program in a batch system. But job has a different meaning in other operating system types. A job is a unit of work. A program in execution can be called as a job. The job can also be called as a process. These are discussed in detail in the later sections of the chapter.

3.3.2 Multiprogramming

We will see a simple analogy, which will help in understanding the concept of multiprogramming. Let us think the grand master in chess is playing chess with 5 players simultaneously. The grand master makes the first move with the first player. The first player takes sometime for making the move. Let us say he waits.

So the master player goes to attend the second player. He makes a move here too. Now the player 2 also waits. In a similar way the master player attends all the other remaining players and finally comes to the player 1 and attends him. This creates a scenario in which a master player is simultaneously playing with 5 players. This simple analogy can be correlated with the multiprogramming operating system. The master player is like CPU. The players are jobs or processes to be attended by the CPU. In this type of operating system several jobs can be executed simultaneously.

Let us consider job J1 is initially assigned to CPU. While this job is being executed, it may need some data to be given as input. It waits for the user to type the data. The human to his maximum speed takes one second to input the data. During this time the CPU has to wait (1 sec is 1000 ms which cannot be tolerated). During this time the CPU can be assigned to job J2 by the operating system. While J2 is waiting for an I/O operation, the CPU can be switched to some other job. This technique can be repeated for all the jobs in a round-robin fashion. In this fashion it will attend all the jobs. The CPU will never be idle. This multiprogramming concept can be understood with the help of the following diagram in Fig. 3.2.

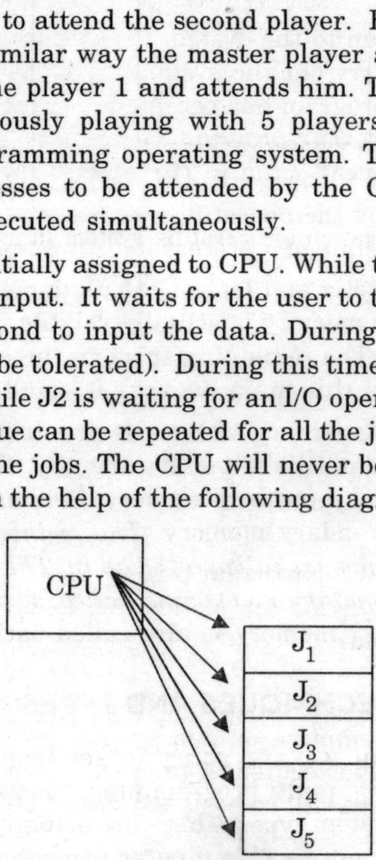

Fig. 3.2 Multiprogramming CPU is switched over among the jobs J_1 to J_5

In this type jobs are waiting in queue. They are ready to run. They are assigned CPU generally by the operating system. However, there is lots of CPU scheduling algorithms available, which will be discussed in the later sections of this chapter. This operating system technique greatly increases the performance. The CPU is not left idle. The CPU utilization is more, compared to the other techniques. CPU utilization is a measure performance of the CPU.

3.3.3 Time Sharing

This is a special type of multiprogramming. The concept is same as that of multiprogramming with a slight change in switching the jobs. The CPU is switched over the jobs based on the time slice or time quantum. In this type each job is given a fixed amount of time interval called time slice. After the expiry of the time slice the CPU will be switched to the next job by the operating system. In similar way the jobs are switched at fixed time intervals. This technique is highly interactive. This technique gives even better CPU utilization than the multiprogramming. This is also called multitasking. The switching of jobs is called contexts witching.

There are other important operating system types available like SPOOLING (Simultaneous Peripheral Operations On Line), Distributed operating systems, Real time operating systems and Single user operating system.

3.4 PROCESS

The user submits a program to the system for execution. In order to run the program the operating system has to carry out the system activities like I/O management, memory management and others. The program has become an active entity. (It was a passive entity before it is given for execution). *The program in execution is called a process. It is a unit of work in a system. It is a system activity. The process can also be called as a job.*

A process can be created by the operating system. The processes will be in any one of the following listed states. The state of a process indicates the current activity of a particular process. The states are:

1. Ready state
2. Running state
3. Waiting state

Ready state indicates that a particular process is ready to be executed by the processor.

Running state indicates that a particular process is being executed *i.e.*, the instructions are being executed.

Waiting state indicates that a particular process is waiting for activity to be completed. It may be any system activity like I/O completion. After undergoing all the necessary states the processes will be terminated.

3.4.1 Context Switching

The processes can be preemptive or non preemptive. In multiprogramming various processes will be simultaneously executed. A process, which is assigned CPU, will be taken away and some other new process will be assigned the CPU. After some time the old process will be attended by the CPU.

The CPU is switched among the processes. This is called *context switching*. During context switching the status of the CPU has to be saved. This is necessary for future resumption of that process. The status of any process can be stored in a data structure called *Process Control Block (PCB)*.

3.4.2 Threads

Threads are alternative to processes for certain kinds of concurrent applications. This has less over head. It avoids overheads due to process management, scheduling, if it were processes used for concurrent applications.

Consider two processes P_1 & P_2. Let us say, they are created for a same application. They share the same code and data. They also share the same resources like CPU registers and stacks. If context switching is done between these two processes, the status of the resources are unnecessarily saved and resumed in multiprogramming. The overhead is high due to this. This can be avoided if we group this co-operating process together. This leads to a new entity called 'Thread'. It is a unit of concurrency. The threads share same code and data. Under any process these threads will be clubbed. The associated processes which share the code data and other resources for concurrent applications can be grouped under a process. The associated processes are called threads.

The concept of threads has little resemblance to classes in object oriented programming languages. In a class the data and its member functions are grouped. Here too the threads and its data are grouped. This may not be a best analogy but too some extent it will help in understanding the concepts of threads. The following diagram will give a clear idea about threads.

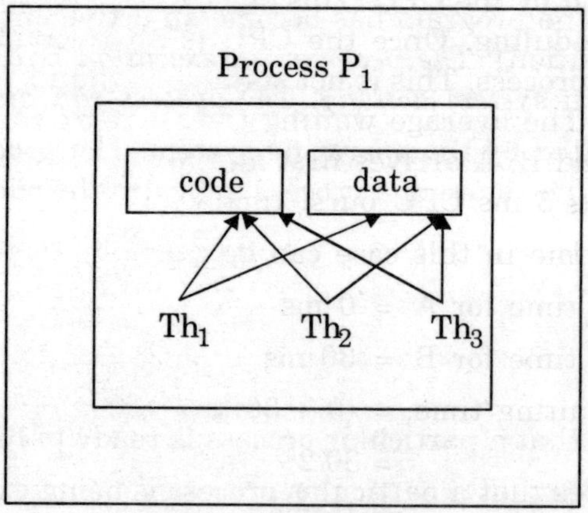

Fig. 3.3 Threads

$P_1 \rightarrow$ Process

Th_1, Th_2, Th_3 $\rightarrow$ Threads

Threads are though grouped under processes; they almost behave like processes only. There is no PCB and its related functions. See Fig. 3.3. (P_2 is not shown).

3.5 SCHEDULING

Scheduling is the one of the important function of the operating system. The resources must be scheduled for better performance. In this section the resource CPU is taken for consideration. The operating system types like multiprogramming and time sharing necessitate CPU scheduling. The idea is to increase the CPU utilization. The CPU should not be kept idle. The CPU must be scheduled in such a way the maximum CPU utilization is obtained. The CPU scheduling can be also called as short term scheduling.

In the multi programming technique the CPU will be waiting for the completion of an I/O operation, during that time the CPU will be switched to some other new job in the job queue. The operating system switches the CPU to the new job. While switching the operating system saves the status of the old job separately in order to resume it later. This is called context switching. This can happen during an interrupt also.

There can be preemptive and nonpreemptive scheduling in CPU scheduling. If the CPU has been allocated to a process, the process voluntarily only will release the CPU under nonpreemptive scheduling. In case of preemptive scheduling the CPU can be released by the operating system from the process if any situation warrants.

The queue will be keeping the jobs to be allocated to CPU. This is generally available in the main memory. It is clear that a queue is data structure, which works in First Come First Served Basis (FCFS). Generally queues are used in CPU scheduling.

There are some performance measures for the CPU scheduling algorithms like CPU utilization, throughput, waiting time, response time and others. These will help in assessing the performance of the CPU scheduling algorithms. Some CPU scheduling algorithms are discussed hereunder.

3.5.1 First Come First Served Scheduling (FCFS)

In this algorithm the job comes first will be served first by the CPU. The queue will be keeping the jobs to be served by the CPU. This algorithm is very simple to implement. This is nonpreemptive type scheduling. Once the CPU is allotted to a process, it will only be released by that particular process. This is not suitable for multi programming, time sharing type of operating systems. The average waiting time is more in this type of scheduling. If there are two jobs say A and B. A arrives first and it wants 30 ms CPU burst time, and B arrives second and it wants 5 ms CPU burst time.

The average waiting time in this case can be calculated as follows:

The waiting time for A = 0 ms

The waiting time for B = 30 ms

The average waiting time = (0 + 30)/2

= 30/2

= 15 ms.

Consider process B arrives first and A arrives second:

The waiting time for B = 0 ms

The waiting time for B = 5 ms

The average waiting time = (0 + 5)/2

= 5/2

= 2.5 ms.

From this simple example we can understand the average waiting time is optimal in this type of scheduling.

3.5.2 Shortest Job First Scheduling (SJF)

This is a CPU scheduling algorithm. The criterion for selection of jobs, is shortest CPU burst time. The job, which is having shortest CPU burst time, will be attended first by the CPU. This algorithm can be understood as shortest remaining time first because the CPU is allotted to the job, which is having shortest remaining time among the available jobs. This algorithm is optimal compared to the other algorithms. This can be either preemptive or nonpreemptive. The average waiting time is less than first come first served algorithm. The difficulty lies in estimating the burst time of next job.

There are other scheduling algorithms like priority scheduling, round robin scheduling and others. The priority scheduling algorithm selects jobs based on some priority. In this each job is associated with a priority. The job, which is having highest priority, is given the CPU. Sometimes in this algorithm the low priority job will never get the CPU. This problem is called starvation. This can be solved by gradually incrementing the priority of the low priority job. This is called aging.

The round robin algorithm works on round robin fashion. Jobs from 1 to n will be attended and then it will be repeated from beginning in a round robin fashion. This algorithm is best suitable in time sharing type operating system. We know in time sharing system each job will be given the CPU for a particular time quantum only. In similar a way this algorithm also works. This is preemptive type of algorithm.

3.5.3 Priority Scheduling

This is another scheduling algorithm, in which the CPU is allocated based on some priority attached to each job. In this algorithm, each job is attached with some priority. The job with highest priority will be assigned the CPU. The priority to a particular job can be assigned on some criteria. For example the student jobs will have least priority and the system processes will be having more priority. The priority is actually a number. The numbers are used to represent the priority are 1,2,3,4, etc. The number 1 will have first priority, and the number 4 will have last priority in this case.

This scheduling can be either preemptive or non preemptive. Assume the CPU is executing a process. Another new process is arriving the queue. Its priority is checked with the priority of the process being executed. If it is higher than the process in execution, then the newly arrived process will be assigned the CPU by preempting the old process in case of preemptive scheduling. But in case of nonpreemptive scheduling the newly arrived process will be placed at the top of the queue.

Some times this will lead to indefinite block of CPU even though it is ready to run in case of preemptive scheduling. This is due to the prevention of CPU by the higher priority process to the lower priority processes. This indefinite blocking is called starvation. This problem can be solved by a technique called aging. Aging is technique to increase the priority of the processes, waiting for a long time, gradually. At one time the lower priority processes will also become a higher priority due to this technique. This is very similar to seniority of an employee in an organization because of his/her experience.

There are some more scheduling algorithms for CPU scheduling. The important few algorithms only discussed in this book. The readers are advised to refer the books on operating systems for further references, if necessary.

3.6 MEMORY MANAGEMENT

Memory management is one important function of the operating system. The memory for a computer system can be both main memory and secondary memory. How effectively these memories are managed to yield better throughput. The throughput is a performance measure. It can be defined as the number of jobs done over a particular time interval. When the memory is effectively managed the probability of increasing the throughput is higher. The necessity for effectively handling the memory arises is due to the various operating system techniques like multiprogramming, multitasking, and etc. The execution of any program is done at the main memory. The secondary memory serves as the back store, which will generally keep the data and supplies the data to the main memory whenever necessary.

We will see about swapping before seeing the other memory management techniques.

3.6.1 Swapping

In multiprogramming like techniques a process can be preempted and some other process can be brought in for execution. We can understand that from this, a process can be brought into the main memory from the secondary memory and also a process can be brought out from main memory into secondary memory. This is called swapping. The method of bringing a process into the main memory from the secondary memory is called swapping in. The method of bringing a process out of the main memory into secondary memory is called swapping out.

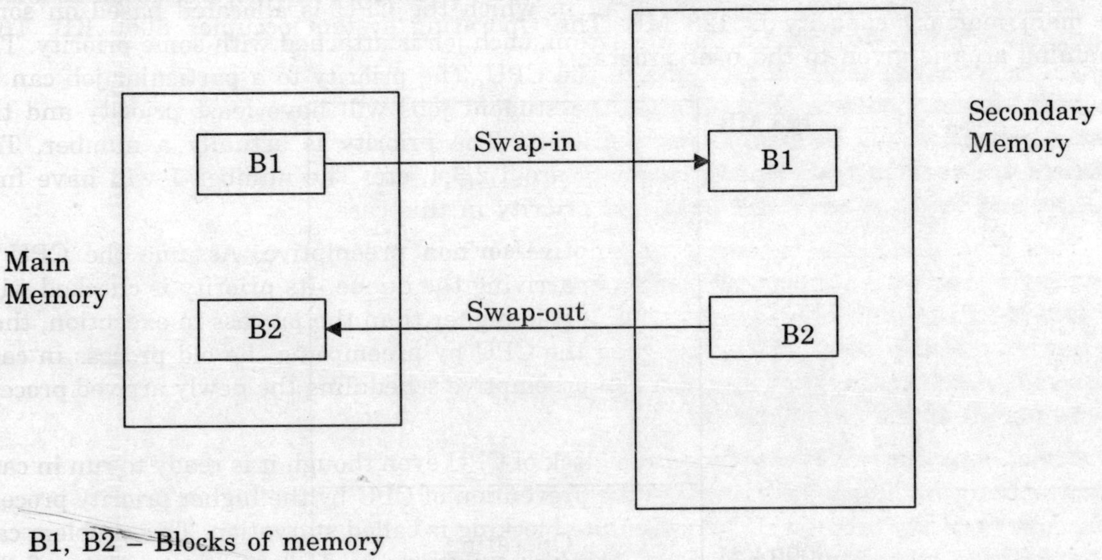

Fig. 3.4 Swapping

The Fig. 3.4 swapping shows how swapping is done from main memory to secondary memory and vice versa. Here B_1, B_2 refer to blocks of memory or these can be any memory related entity. These may be processes also. Mostly processes are swapped. Swapping keeps the most useful processes in the memory. The operating system does the swapping of processes.

3.6.2 Memory Allocation Schemes

Allocation of memory to various requests is one of the major activities of the operating system. In this section we will see about some memory allocation schemes. They are listed below:

1. Single partition allocation
2. Multiple partition allocation

These memory allocation schemes are for only for the main memory. The allocation schemes are useful in handling the main memory effectively *i.e.*, to best utilize the main memory.

3.6.3 Single Partition Allocation

This is a simple memory management scheme. The entire main memory is given to the disposal of the user. In fact there is no division of the memory. No specialized software or hardware is needed for this memory management scheme. This scheme has lot of disadvantages and it does not provide any services.

There is another scheme, which is an extension of the previous scheme. This has two divisions. One for the operating system and the second for the user programs. The lower portion is allotted for the operating system. The remaining portion can be used by the user. Lower portion is given to the operating system because the interrupts can be handled effectively in the lower portions only. The organization of the operating system can be shown as it is given in the following diagram Fig. 3.5. Single partition allocation scheme. The main memory capacity is 128 MB. The Operating system occupies 5000 KB. The remaining area is given to the user programs.

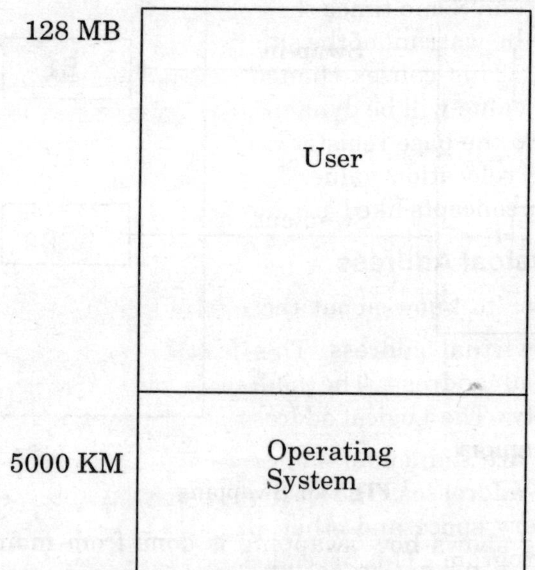

Fig. 3.5 Single partition allocation scheme

In this scheme the operating system must be protected from the user programs. The user code and data should not be placed in the OS area. This can be achieved by a special hard ware mechanism. This is called base—limit register scheme.

In this scheme there are two registers called base and limit registers. The area of operation of a process can be restricted between the base and limit registers. The base register gives the base address to a particular job or process or any entity. The base address is actually the starting address of the memory for a process. The limit register gives the range in which the process can work. Let us see an example.

Base address value = 8000

Limit register value = 0500

Process = P1

In this case the process P1 has the base address as 8000 and the limit register's address is 500. According to this situation the P1 can occupy up to 8000 from 8500. The process P1 cannot occupy memory other than the specified area. Otherwise it will be illegal operation. If there is an illegal reference then there will be *OS trap*, which will stop the process from execution. The legal address should be greater than the base address and should be less than the base + limit address value.

Legal Address > = Base Address AND < (Base Address + Limit Address)

This is how the hardware mechanism gives protection. Sometimes the CPU gets locked into an infinite loop in any process due to some errors. This will lead to starvation for the waiting jobs and some times dead lock like complications. This can be avoided by employing a timer. After the timer value the process will be compulsorily release the CPU. This method will be much suitable for time sharing OS technique. In time sharing the jobs are given particular time interval. After the expiry that time interval the control will be taken back from that job.

In the single partition allocation scheme, some times there is a possibility for changing the address of operating system. Some times the operating system code may be swapped out and swapped in due to some the warrant of the situations. So the occupation of memory by the operating system may vary. This causes change in the base register values for the use programs. The base register value will be dynamically changed due to the dynamic nature of the operating system code. So the base register becomes the relocation register. It keeps the value, which is actually the relocation value. So the base register can better be called as relocation register. The other concepts like base and limit register mechanisms are same only.

Logical Address and Physical Address

At this point, it is better to know about the logical address and physical addresses.

The logical address is virtual address. This is user defined or programmer defined address. This is not the real address. The addresses, which the users manipulate, are actually logical addresses only. The Logical addresses can also be called as virtual addresses.

The physical addresses are the actual addresses. These are real addresses. These are operating system generated addresses. The user may not know these addresses. Based on the availability of the memory space and other situations the operating system generates the address for the user program. This is called as the physical address. The physical addresses can also be called as real addresses.

Consider the user-defined instruction has the address 1000. The user program is normally addressed from 0 onwards. The base register value is 4000 and the limit register value is 1500. From this situation we can understand the following:

Logical address = 1000

Base address = 4000

Limit register value = 1500.

The limit register value is nothing but the range *i.e.*, the user program can occupy the memory from 4000 to 5500 (4000 + 1500 = 5500). So the operating system generates the address for the given user instruction as 4000 + 1000 = 5000. This address is actually physical address. This is generated by the operating system. This is well within the specified limit. If the base register value is changed then the physical address will also change.

Multiple Partition Allocation

This memory allocation scheme has multiple partitions as its name implies. This scheme is more suitable for multi programming type operating systems. In this case the main memory is partitioned according to the jobs or process available for execution. The main memory is initially loaded with the operating system. The remaining memory is free. This can be considered as a large hole freely available for allocation. ***Any particular free space of memory can be called as a hole.***

Let us consider an example for multiple partition allocation scheme. We will see how the processes are allocated under this scheme.

For example, 3.1

Processes	Memory	Time units
P1	1000 KB	5
P2	4000 KB	3
P3	2000 KB	4
P4	5000 KB	6

In the example situation there are five processes P1, P2, P3, and P4 and the corresponding memory requirements are also given. The time unit required for each process is also given in the chart. The processes are ready for execution. Initially the main memory is occupied with 2000 KB of memory. The remaining memory is for user programs. The user processes are allotted the memory as per their requirements. The allocation under this scheme is shown in the Fig. 3.6. The main memory capacity is 10000 KB. The processes are allotted according to the size. Due to that only P1, P2 and P3 are able to allotted memory. The processes P4 could not be allotted. There is also a hole of size 1000 KB, which cannot be allotted to the process P4. The required size is 5000 KB.

The situation will change after 3 time units because the process completes its execution. Now the 4000 KB of memory is released. This can be used for the waiting processes. This situation is shown in the following Fig. 3.7. Now there are two holes. The newly created hole is of size 4000 KB, due to the release of the process P2. The other hole is of size 1000 KB, which is already available. These are two separate holes and not contiguously (adjacently) placed. Now the process P4 cannot be given access to the memory because the holes are sufficient enough to accommodate the process. If the two holes are contiguously available, probably the process can be allotted.

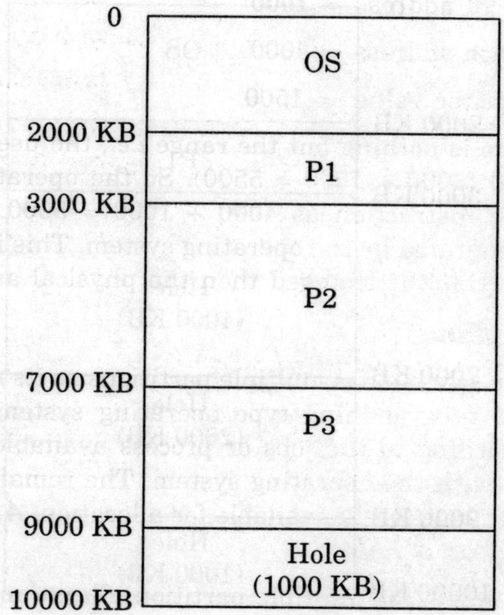

Fig. 3.6 Multiple partition memory allocation 1

After 3 time units

Fig. 3.7 Multiple partition memory allocation 2

After the expiry 4 time units, the process P3 completes its execution. So there will be new hole of size 2000 KB. This situation is shown in the Fig. 3.8. Now the holes are together available. The process P4 can be allotted memory. This situation is shown in the Fig. 3.9. Now all the waiting processes are attended.

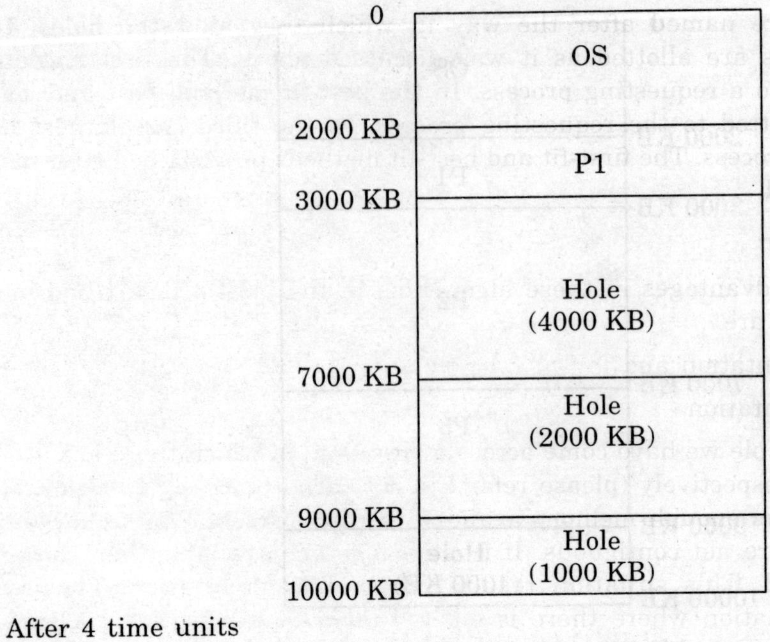

Fig. 3.8 Multiple partition memory allocation 3

Fig. 3.9 Multiple partition memory allocation 4

There are some algorithms available for the allocation of holes to the processes. These are given below:

1. First-fit
2. Best-fit
3. Worst-fit

These algorithms are named after the way in which they allot the holes. In the first-fit method the holes are allotted as it was discussed above. The first encountered suitable hole is allotted to a requesting process. In the best-fit method, best and smallest hole suitable hole is allotted to the requesting process. In the third case largest hole is allotted to a requesting process. The first-fit and best-fit methods prove to be better methods over the worst-fit method.

External Fragmentation

There are some disadvantages in these algorithms in the multiple partition memory allocation schemes. They are

1. External fragmentation and
2. Internal fragmentation

In the previous example we have come across a situation, in which there are two holes of sizes 4000 and 1000 respectively (please refer Fig. 3.7). The process P4 is requesting a hole of size 5000. There is enough memory available for the process P4, but it cannot be allotted since the holes are not contiguous. If it were together available then the process could have been allotted. This situation results external fragmentation. The external fragmentation is the situation where there is enough memory available for a particular request, and it cannot be attended because the memory is not contiguously available.

Compaction

The external fragmentation problem can be solved by compaction. The major problem in external fragmentation is memory is not available contiguously. If the memory is available contiguously then the external fragmentation problem can be solved. The method of bringing together the available free spaces can be called as compaction. This is to bring the holes together to make the available memory contiguously. This can be achieved either moving the holes down or up *i.e.*, to move to a particular end. The Fig. 3.10.1 gives clear picture about compaction. From the figure we can understand that there are two free holes hole1 and hole 2 of sizes 4000 KB and 1000 KB respectively. There are also two processes P1 and P2 are inside the memory and are being executed. This situation will lead to external fragmentation. Suppose there is another process requesting a hole of size of 5000 KB and this cannot be allotted by the operating system. This is due to external fragmentation. Though sufficient memory is available, the request cannot be attended. Compacting together the holes can solve this problem. This is shown in the Fig. 3.10.2. (Please compare the situations before and after compaction in the figures).

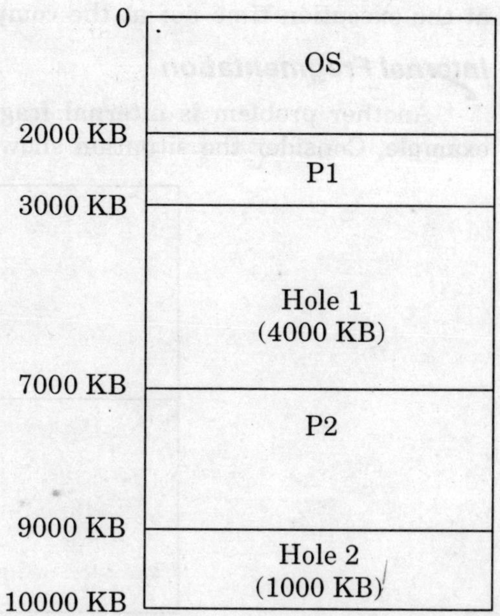

Fig. 3.10(a) External fragmentation

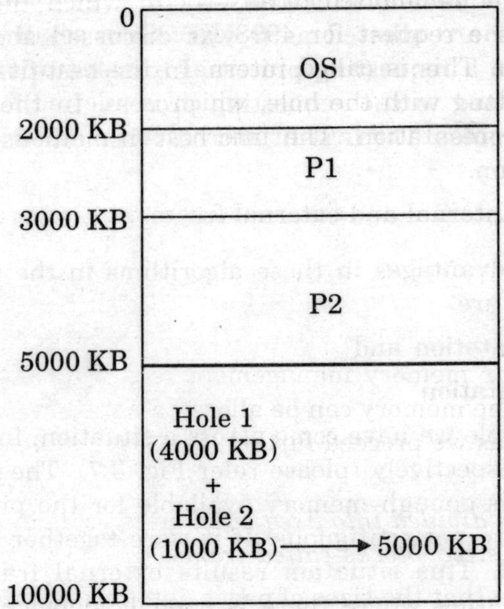

Fig. 3.10(b) Compaction of holes

There is lot of methods to compact together the available storage. Swapping can also be compaction so that compaction can be done effectively. The compaction can be done provided that dynamic relocation is permitted in the system. The compaction must be done at the execution time not at the compile time. Compaction cannot be done statically.

Internal Fragmentation

Another problem is internal fragmentation. This can be understood by the following example. Consider the situation shown below:

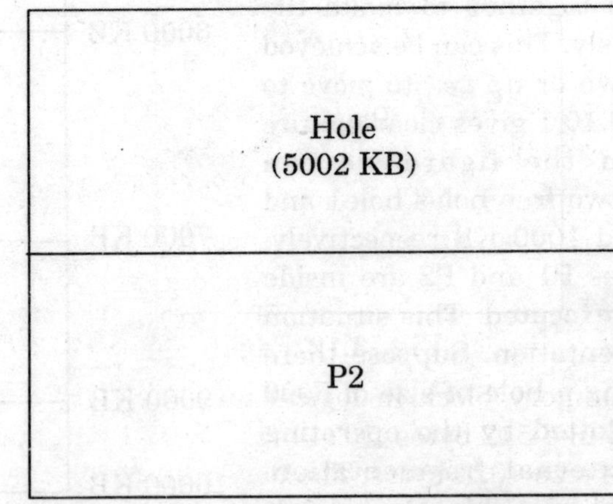

Fig. 3.11 Memory allocation leads to internal fragmentation

From the Fig. 3.11, we can understand that there is a hole of size 5002 KB. There is a request for a hole of size of 4998 KB for a process Pn. If this request is allotted then there will be a hole of size 4 KB. This hole is very small in size. The overhead involved in maintaining the hole by operating is same for all sorts of holes. This overhead is expensive because this small will not be allotted to any process. So operating system attaches this portion also along with the request for 4998 KB. So a small portion of memory will be unused in the process Pn. This is called internal fragmentation. Small-unused portion of memory left internally, along with the hole, which is allotted for a particular request, can be called as internal fragmentation. The internal fragmentation can be solved to some extent by the segmentation.

The solutions to the internal and external fragmentation problems are discussed in the subsequent sections.

3.7 PAGING

The paging is another memory management technique, which avoids the problem of external fragmentation. The memory can be allocated non-contiguously for any process. This we will come understand as we proceed further. The paging method is widely used in many operating systems.

The logical memory is divided into fixed sized blocks called pages. The physical memory is also divided into fixed sized blocks called frames.

It is important to note that the sizes of pages and frames are equal. The frames can also be called as page frames. The pages are logical entities that contain information. The frames are physical entities that contain pages. The physical and logical memory concepts are already discussed in the 3.6.3. These terms are pertinent to the main memory. *The secondary memory is also divided into fixed sized blocks of same in size with pages or frames.* The pages are in the logical memory. The frames are in the physical memory. The logical memory is contiguous. The physical memory may not be contiguous. This is reason for paging to eliminate the problem of external fragmentation. It avoids the need for dynamic memory allocation.

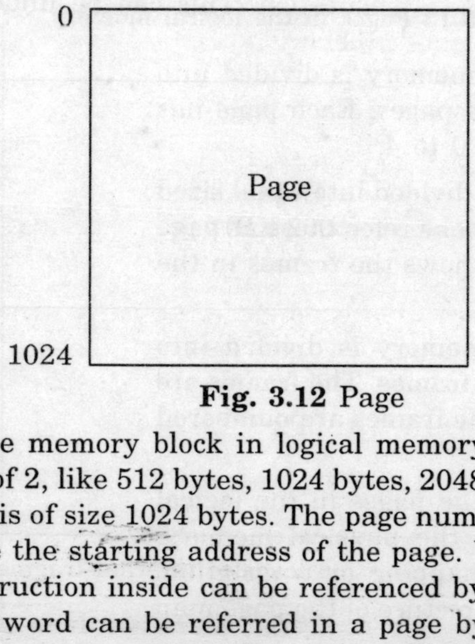

Fig. 3.12 Page

A page is fixed size memory block in logical memory. The pages can be of any size, which should be power of 2, like 512 bytes, 1024 bytes, 2048 bytes and the like. The Fig. 3.12 shows a simple page. It is of size 1024 bytes. The page number is used to generally reference a page. It is almost like the starting address of the page. We can also say that as the base address. A word or instruction inside can be referenced by the displacement or offset from the base address. So a word can be referred in a page by adding the displacement value with the base address *i.e.*, page number. The following notations are used for the discussions about paging.

P – Page number
D – Page displacement
F – Frame number
D – Frame displacement

The paging is nothing but mapping the pages into frames. The page in the logical address space is mapped into a frame in the physical address space, can be called as paging.

The translation of pages into frames is done with the help of a table called page table. It helps the mapping. We will see with an example how paging is done. In paging there are three components as listed below:

1. Pages in the logical memory
2. Page map table
3. Frames in the main memory.

The logical memory is divided into pages. These are user-defined addresses. The following Fig. 3.13 shows how the pages are divided in the logical address space.

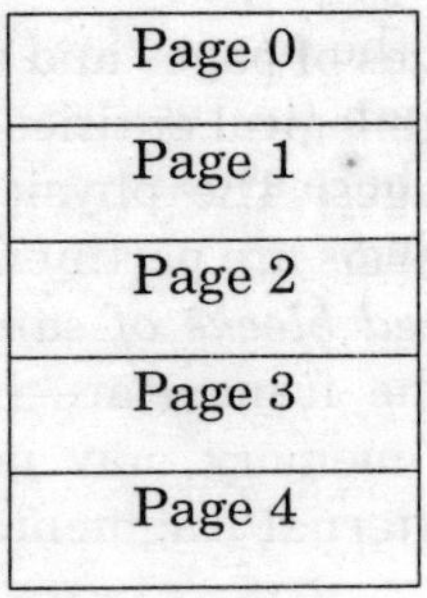

Fig. 3.13 Pages in the logical memory

In this example the logical memory is divided into equal sized pages. There are five pages. Each page has a page number. These are from 0 to 4.

The physical memory is also divided into equal sized blocks called frames. Some textbooks refer these as page frames. The following Fig. 3.14 shows the frames in the physical memory.

In this case the physical memory is divided into equal sized frames. There are 11 frames. The frames are having the same size of pages. The frames are numbered from 0 to 10.

The page map table maps the pages in the logical address space to the frames in the physical memory. The page map table does the mapping or translation. The following Fig. 3.15 gives the picture of the page map table.

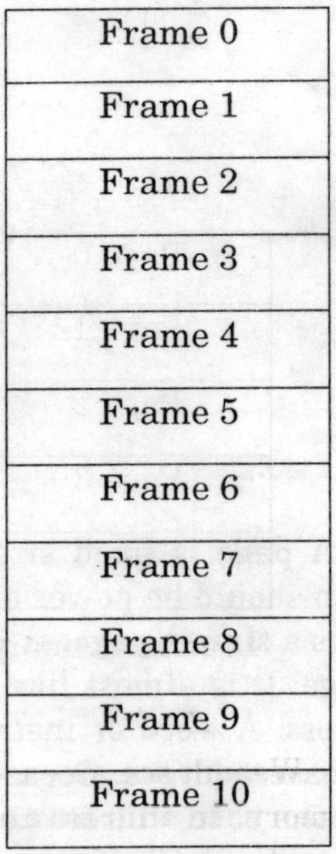

Fig. 3.14 Frames in the physical memory

Pages → Frame

Pages	Frame
0	5
1	2
2	4
3	1
4	6

Fig. 3.15 Page map table

It is evident how the pages are mapped into frames through the page map table. The page 0 is mapped to the frame 5. Similarly all the other pages are mapped to corresponding frames. All the above functions together constitute the complete paging model. The Fig. 3.16 gives the view of a paging model, which is nothing but the club of all the above-discussed components. In the physical memory, pages filled into the frames. Actually frames were considered to be free before loading the pages. The frame numbers are given besides to the pages in the figure in the first column (in reality there is no column and this is given for the understanding to the readers). There are some frames free, which will be used in future. This is the concept behind the paging.

Logical memory

Page 0
Page 1
Page 2
Page 3
Page 4

Page table

Page	Frame
0	5
1	2
2	4
3	0
4	6

Physical memory

Frame	Content
0	Page 3
1	
2	Page 1
3	
4	Page 2
5	Page 0
6	Page 4
7	
8	
9	
10	

Fig. 3.16 A paging model

We will see an example how an instruction in a page is mapped to a frame in the physical memory. In this case, consider the page size as 8 words. There are 5 pages and 11 frames. Consider the 3rd instruction or word in the page 1. The logical address is 1 and the displacement (D) is 3. The page is mapped to 2nd frame. The frame is having the number as 2. So the physical address is 8. So the logical address 1 is mapped to the physical address 8 (base address). The displacement D is added with the base address. The resultant physical address is 8 + 3 = 11. So the 3rd instruction in the page is mapped to the physical address 11.

The other advantage in paging, there can be common pages for few user processes. Such pages can be shared. These are shared pages.

The paging technique suffers from internal fragmentation. Unusable portion of memory (usually small in size), within the partially filled page is called internal fragmentation. This is due to the fixed sized nature of the pages. The nature of the problem and its solution segmentation are discussed in the next section.

3.8 SEGMENTATION

The problem with the paging is, it does not reflect the user's view of memory. Pages are fixed sized partitions irrespective of the memory arrangement of the user program. In reality the user program is not ordered linear array of words. It has different logical program entities. A program generally may have main program, one or more subroutines of different sizes. So a user program may be considered as set of procedures of different sizes. These are not ordered also. The procedures can be treated as segments. Keeping this in mind, a program can be considered as unordered collection of segments of different sizes. Consider the following example:

Main program – 200 KB
Subroutine 1 – 400 KB
Subroutine 2 – 300 KB and
Subroutine 3 – 600 KB

In this program there are four segments of different sizes. If this program is submitted under paging system, all these have to be divided into fixed sized blocks, which in fact violate the very nature of the program. It leads problems like internal fragmentation and others.

The segmentation method gives solution to this problem. It keeps the segments as such. That is why the name segmentation. This scheme considers the user program as, an unordered set of variable sized segments. These segments correspond to the different sized logical program units like procedures, data objects and other program segments.

In the segmented memory system the logical memory is divided into segments of different size. The segmentation maps the segments in the logical address space into the physical memory. There is nothing called frames in the physical memory. At this point it is worth to note, this memory allocation is very similar to the multiple partition allocation scheme. (Please refer section 3.6.4).

The other concepts are very similar to the concepts of paging. Each segment has a segment number, which is like the base address of the segment. There is also displacement or offset available, which is useful in address translation. The concept of mapping is very similar to the concept of paging. There is also a Segment Mapping Table (SMT) available, which is used for segment translation.

The segment number is used to choose segment register, which is nothing but the relocation register. A segment contains a base register, which points to the starting of the segment. It has also a length register, which tells the length of the segment. So it is clear that each segment has a base and limit registers.

The segmentation scheme to some extent is similar to the multiple partition scheme. So it also suffers external fragmentation. There will be holes will be available in a non-contiguous manner, which cannot be effectively used. This external fragmentation problem can be solved by compaction.

In operating systems paging and segmentations are used. The combination of this called paged segmentation is also used in some operating systems.

3.9 VIRTUAL MEMORY

This section discusses about the virtual memory concepts and also mechanisms to implement the same. Let us see a simple analogy.

I generally take Rs.100/- for daily expenses from my wife. My bank balance is Rs.1 Lakh. I have money Rs.100/-, which is sufficient for my daily expenses. If need money I can take more money from the bank. So I have a feeling that I have Rs.1 Lakh for my disposal, which is quite large money, and I can go for other expenses. Whenever demand arises I will take from the bank. In reality I have only Rs.100 in my pocket, which is sufficient for my expenses at a particular time in a day.

This situation can be related to concept of virtual memory. The money in the pocket can be related to the real physical memory. The money in bank can be related to the back store *i.e.*, secondary memory. The demand can be analogous to special type of paging technique called demand paging.

The virtual memory (virtual means something not in real) allows the programmer to have a feeling that large amount of memory available for his disposal, though it is not available. Normally the physical memory is less in size. If the user program requires memory larger than the physical memory, then the virtual memory can be used. *The virtual memory maps the large logical address space into small physical memory space*. In virtual memory some of the memory is simulated in the secondary memory. The virtual memory tries to map the logical address to physical address. If the physical memory is not sufficient then it brings in some pages from the secondary memory by releasing some unwanted pages from the main memory. The programmer is relieved off from these constraints. He thinks a huge amount of memory is available for his disposal.

The Fig. 3.17 shows simple model of virtual memory system. The logical memory is divided into pages. The physical memory is divided into frames. The mapping is done with the help of page table. The virtual memory system is very similar to paging system except one difference. In virtual memory system paging is done with swapping, is the difference from paging system. The operating system checks whether the required page is available in the main memory, if it is not available then it will swap the required page from the secondary memory. We can under stand the functions involved in the virtual memory system, from the Fig. 3.17.

The virtual memory allows many processes to be executed simultaneously. It increases the CPU utilization. The degree of multi programming is also increased due to virtual memory. This can be implemented using paging, to be more precise, demand paging.

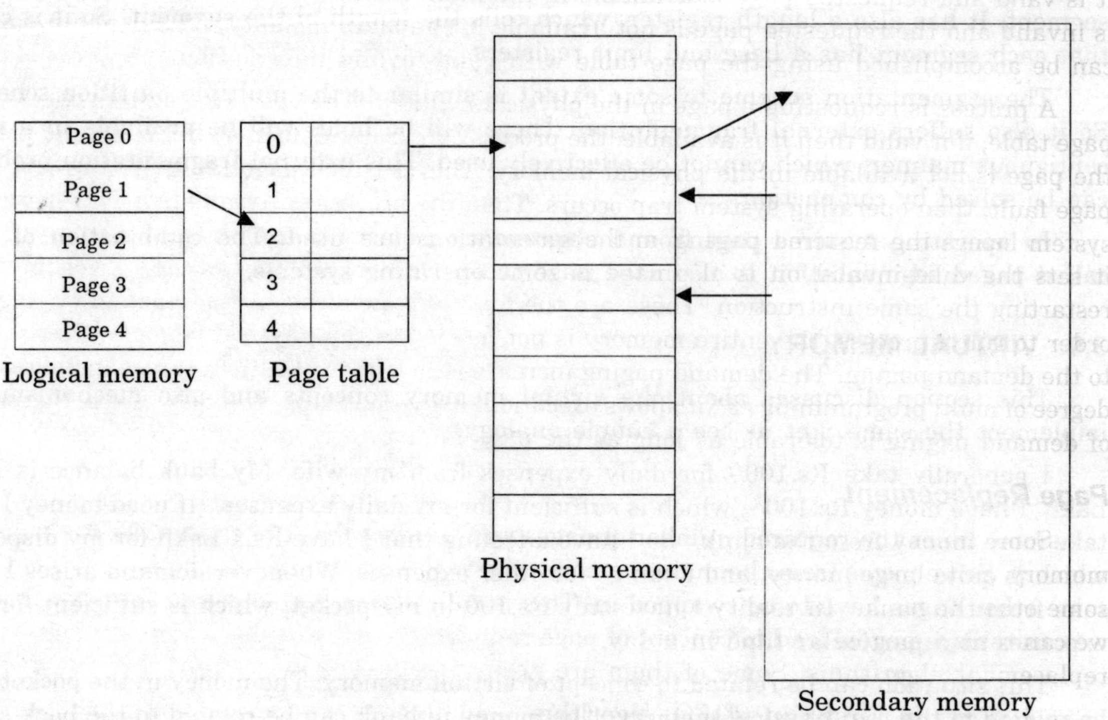

Fig. 3.17 Virtual memory system

Demand Paging

The virtual memory can be implemented by demand paging. The demand paging system is used to implement the virtual memory. The demand paging is also a paging system with swapping. The page will be swapped only when there is a demand. This paging is very dynamic in nature. This entire paging activity is done only on demands. All the components discussed in the virtual memory system are also available and functions are also same. The paging is done only on demand. The page table is slightly modified to carry out the demand paging. The page table has one more entity 'present bit' or valid-invalid bit. This is shown in the Fig. 3.18.

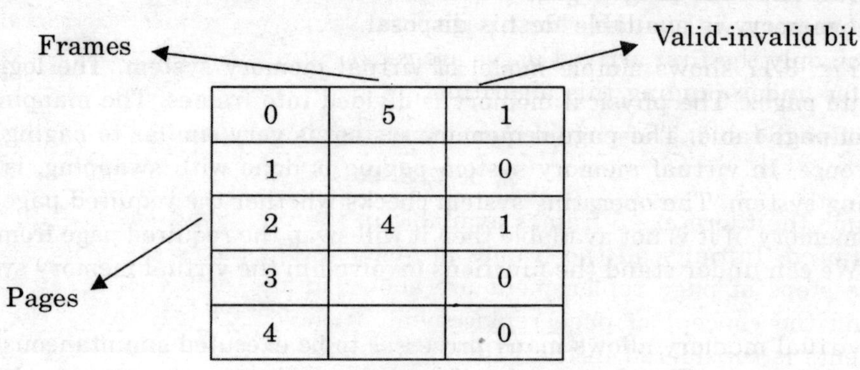

Fig. 3.18 Page table in demand paging

The valid-invalid bit is an indicator, which is used to indicate whether the required page is available the physical memory. It can have either '0' or 1 value. If it is '1' means, it is valid and requested page is available in the main memory. If the value is '0' means it is invalid and the requested page is not available in the main memory. The demand paging can be accomplished using the page table with valid-invalid information.

A process is requesting a page in the physical memory. The operating system checks the page table, if it valid then it is available, the process can proceed further. If it is invalid means the page is not available in the physical memory. This is called page fault. When there is a page fault, then operating system trap occurs. Then the process is terminated. The operating system brings the required page from the secondary memory to the physical memory. Then it sets the valid-invalid bit to '1' in the page table. Once again the process is resumed by restarting the same instruction. These are the functions involved in the demand paging. In order to run a process, the entire memory is not needed in the physical memory. This is due to the demand paging. The demand paging increases the CPU utilization. It also increases the degree of multi programming *i.e.*, it allows execution more number of processes. The performance of demand paging is tolerable as long as the page fault rate is low.

Page Replacement

Some times the required number of pages will be exceeding the capacity of the physical memory. Some pages from the main memory (physical memory) have to be swapped out and some other pages have to be swapped in. This is called page replacement. On what criteria we can replace pages, lead to concept of page replacement algorithms. There are many page replacement algorithms. Some of them are given hereunder.

1. First In First Out (FIFO) algorithm
2. Optimal algorithm
3. Least Recently Used (LRU) algorithm
4. Least Frequently Used (LFU) algorithm
5. Most Frequently Used (LFU) algorithm and others.

All these algorithms are determining what are the pages can be replaced. That is motivation behind these algorithms. Some algorithms are discussed in this section.

First In First Out (FIFO) Algorithm

This algorithm replaces the pages on simple criteria. It replaces the pages, which arrived first. The first arrived pages are replaced first. The idea is the first arrived page in the main memory will be the oldest page. It may not be required no more. Based on this assumption only the first arrived pages are replaced in this algorithm. We will see a simple example for understanding this algorithm.

Consider the string of page requirements as given below:

2, 5, 7, 8, 9, 4, 6, 6

Assume the there are 5 frames available in the physical memory. The demand paging system is used. Initially all the frames are empty. The pages are mapped making a page fault. The steps of page replacement are shown in the Fig. 3.19(a) to (h) We can easily understand the concept of page replacement in the FIFO algorithm. The string of page requirements is considered in the FIFO order only.

2, 5, 7, 8, 9, 4, 6, 6

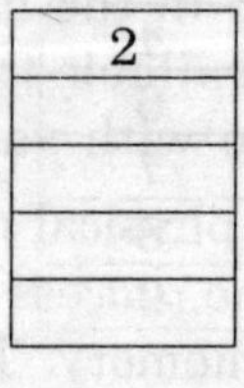

(a) Page 2 is placed

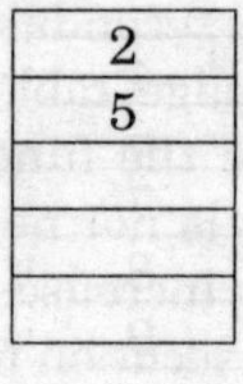

(b) Page 5 is placed

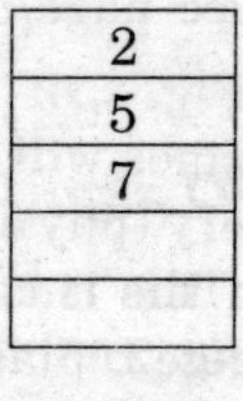

(c) Page 7 is placed

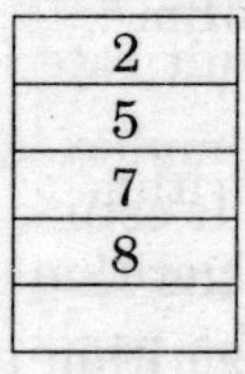

(d) Page 8 is placed

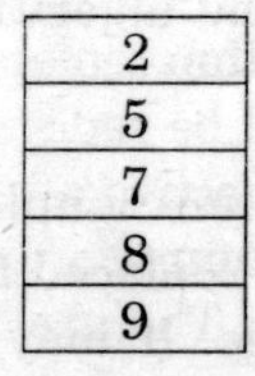

(e) Page 9 is placed

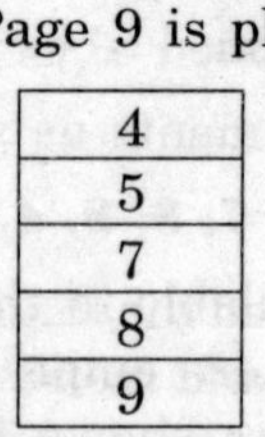

(f) Page 4 replaces page 2

4
6
7
8
9

(g) Page 6 replaces page 5

4
6
7
8
9

(h) No replacement since page 6 is already available

Fig. 3.19

3.19(a) to (h) Page replacement in FIFO algorithm

The pages 2, 5, 7, 8, 9 are placed in the free frames in physical memory. These are actually replaced by page faults. The pages 2, 5 are replaced by 4, 6 respectively because these are first arrived. The page 6 is not replaced because page 6 is already available inside. This algorithm is easy to implement. The performance is not much satisfactory. The disadvantage of this algorithm is page fault rate is high.

The optimal algorithm, as the name implies optimally replaces the pages. It needs the future knowledge about the requirement. It estimates the pages, which will not be used for long time and replacement. It will check the future requirements with the available pages in the physical memory and determine the pages, which will not be used for a long time. This algorithm is better than the FIFO algorithm in performance but it is complex to implement. Estimating the future knowledge is a difficult process in this algorithm.

The Least Recently Used (LRU) algorithm replaces the page, which is used less recently. The page, which is not used for a long time will be replaced in this algorithm. The pages, which are active, will be needed. These will become inactive after some time. This indicates that these will not be further referenced. Based on this assumption these pages are replaced. The LRU algorithm is one of the best global paging algorithms. The algorithm is optimal to 30 to 40 percent.

The other algorithms are working on some criteria for replacing the pages. These are not discussed in detail. The above-discussed algorithms will give an idea about the page replacement concept.

Summary

In this chapter so far we have discussed the fundamentals of operating systems, operating system techniques, process management and memory management. In process management process synchronization, inter process communication and dead locks are not discussed. In the memory management only the main memory management is discussed. The secondary memory management is about the disk management like allocation, scheduling and others. There are also other concepts like file management, security, protection and others, which are not discussed in this book. Only some core concepts are discussed in this book.

QUESTIONS

Part A

1. What is an operating system?
2. What are the functions of operating system?
3. Give few examples for operating systems.
4. What is batch processing?
5. What is multi processing?
6. What is multi programming?
7. What is time-sharing?
8. What is a job?
9. Define a process.
10. What are the differences between a program and a process?
11. What is swapping?
12. What is starvation and how it can be overcome?
13. What is internal fragmentation?
14. What is external fragmentation?
15. What is compaction?
16. What is a page?
17. What the advantages of paging?
18. What is demand paging?
19. What are threads?
20. What are segments?
21. What are logical and physical addresses?
22. What are the differences between multi programming and multi processing?
23. What is a page fault?
24. Write briefly about address translation in non-contiguous allocation.
25. What is thrashing?

Part B

1. Explain the various functions of the operating system in detail.
2. What are various operating system techniques and write brief note on each?
3. Explain about various Job scheduling algorithms in detail.
4. What are the various memory allocation schemes and explain them?
5. Discuss in detail about the main memory management in operating systems.
6. What is virtual memory and explain how the memory management is done using virtual memory?
7. What are the page replacement algorithms available and explain the algorithms with an example?

CHAPTER 4

COMPILERS

Blessed are those who hunger and thirst for righteousness
For they shall be filled.

4.1 INTRODUCTION

In this chapter we are going to discuss the basic concepts of compilers with the help of a simple analogy. The various phases of the compiler are discussed with the help of a simple block diagram. In fact this chapter gives a complete view of the elements involved in the design of a compiler. The design concepts of the compiler phases scanner, parser, intermediate code generator, code optimizer and code generator are discussed in a nutshell. The reader will be able to know the design of a compiler at the end of this chapter.

Translator

Translator is a program, which converts a program written in any source language into any other destination language. The source and destination languages may be any High Level Language (HLL) or Low Level Languages (LLL) like assembly language or machine language.

Compiler

Compiler is a program, which converts a program written in any high level language into an object program.

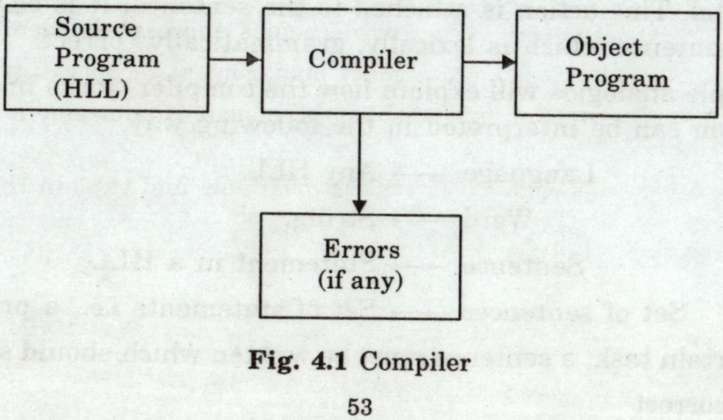

Fig. 4.1 Compiler

Translator can convert one HLL into any other HLL also. But compiler generally converts HLL into LLL only. The compiled programs are eligible for execution. So it is must for any program to be converted into an object program.

Interpreter

Interpreter is also a program in which the code is directly interpreted by the micro code which resides in the control memory of a machine and executed. Micro code is a set of code for an Instruction of a machine, which resides in the cotrol memory of micro-programmed control unit. This micro code generates the control signals for execution. The complex instruction set computers normally runs interpreters.

The following example will help us in understanding concepts of compilers.

Consider the following sentence in English.

HE IS GOING TO SCHOOL.

He ⟶ Subject

is ⟶ Auxillary verb

going ⟶ Verb + ing

to school ⟶ Object.

This simple sentence is syntactically or grammatically correct.

There are some sentences which are not syntactically correct.

Example :

Hi is plaiing.

We can now understand the sentence should be written error free, *i.e.*, lexically (something related to words) correcet in broader sense.

There are also some sentences which are not Grammatically correct.

Example :

The boy is eat the apple.

But the correct sentence is : The boy is eating the apple.

We can also understand the sentence should be written without any grammatical errors.

Okay, we have a sentence, which is lexically and grammatically correct.

Now what is to be done ? The answer is, the boy must do some action, *i.e.*, The boy must go to the hostel. This action is attached to the sentence. It is clear that an action is associated with a sentence which is lexically, grammatically correct.

The above simple analogies will explain how the compiler works in very simpler terms. The above discussion can be interpreted in the following way.

Language ⟶ Any HLL.

Word ⟶ String.

Sentence ⟶ Statement in a HLL.

Set of sentences ⟶ Set of statements *i.e.*, a program in a HLL.

To carryout certain task, a sentence must be written which should satisfy the following:

1. Lexically correct

2. Grammatically (syntactically) correct
3. An action must also be associated. Then,
4. It must be understood by the executor for execution (must be made ready for execution).

In a very similar way, the statement of a program must statisfy the following in a compiler:

1. Lexically correct (Lexical Analyser)
2. Grammatically correct (Syntax Analyser)
3. An action must also be associated (Syntax Directed Translation)
4. It must be understood by the executor for execution. (Code generation and execution)

(**Note** : There is another phase called code optimization which is an optional phase of the compiler)

The reader can relate the above analogy when learning the phases of the compiler in the subsequent sections.

4.2 PHASES OF A COMPILER

The block diagram shows various phases of the compiler clearly.

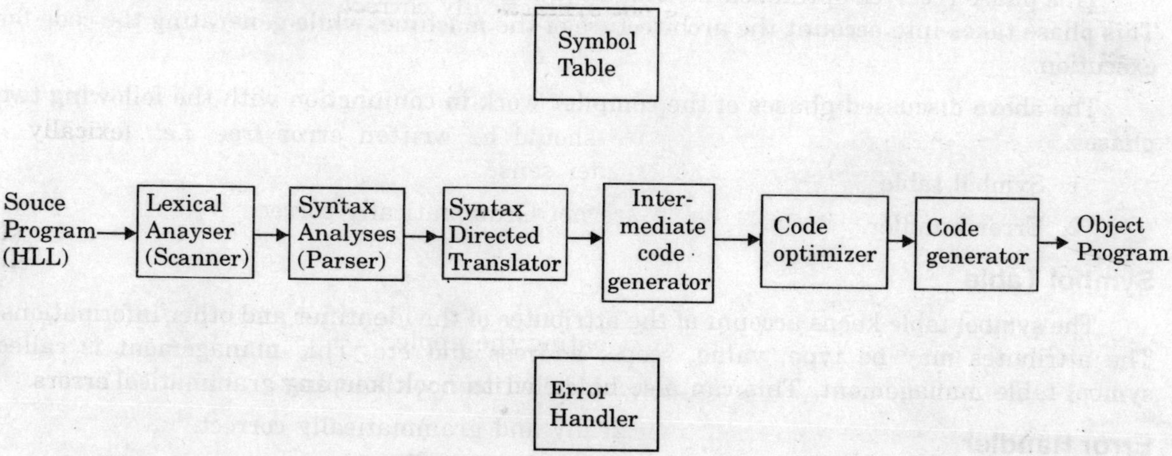

Fig. 4.2 Phases of the compiler

Lexical Analyser

This scans the complete program and generates valid tokens. A token may be a group of characters like keyword, identifier and constant, etc. The lexical analyzer is also called scanner. It also keeps account of line numbers (to indicate the errors in the line numbers, if any) and white spaces.

Syntax Analyser

This receives valid tokens from the scanner and checks them against the grammar and produces the valid syntactical constructs. This is also called parser.

Syntax Directed Translation (SDT)

SDT is a notational frame work, of the valid syntactical constructs received from the syntax analyzer, to make it suitable for intermediate code generation. This attaches actions or rules or subroutines of the grammar.

Intermediate Code Generation

Intermediate code generator receives syntax directed translated syntactical constructs and represent them in any one of the following intermediate codes.

1. Postfix
2. Syntax tree, and
3. Three address code.

Generally three address codes are widely used intermediate codes.

Code Optimizer

The code optimizer receives intermediate codes and improves them considering the factors like memory, execution time and others by applying code optimizing techniques (improving transformations). This phase removes the redundant codes. It is an optional phase.

Code Generator

This phase receives optimized intermediate codes and generates the code for execution. This phase takes into account the architecture of the machine, while generating the code for execution.

The above discussed phases of the compiler work in conjunction with the following two phases:

1. Symbol table
2. Error handler.

Symbol Table

The symbol table keeps account of the attributes of the identifier and other informations. The attributes may be type, value, scope, address and etc. This management is called symbol table management. This can also be called as book keeping.

Error Handler

The error handler invokes error diagonostic routines and generates error messages. It works in conjunction with all the phases to handle the errors at the respective phases.

Phases and Passes

Certain phases of the compiler can be grouped together and can be called as a pass. Generally the first four phases are grouped together and called as Pass 1. This pass 1 includes lexical analyzer, syntax analyzer, syntax directed translation and intermediate code generator phases. This section can be called as front end of the compiler. These are machine independent phases..

The other two phases code optimizer and code generator can together consititute a pass. Generally this is called pass 2. These phases are machine dependent. This pass 2 is called back end of the compiler.

We will discuss each phase of the compiler in detail in the following sections.

4.3 LEXICAL ANALYZER

The lexical analyzer phase generates valid tokens from the scanned source program otherwise generates lexical errors.

The following topics are to be discussed in the lexical analyzer phase.

1. Tokens
2. Regular Expressions
3. Automata Theory

4.3.1 Tokens

The token can be defined as a meaningful group of characters over the character set of the programming language like identifiers, keywords, constants and others.

Example:

Identifier names: **a, comp.**

Keywords: **int, float, char.**

Constants: **3.41, 2000, 444, and**

Punctuation marks:

Language can be defined as set of strings, which are defined over the character set. The character set can be called as "alphabet" and also represented by Σ.

The string can be defined as a set of characters defined over the character set. The operations possible are concatenation, comparison, copying and others.

The operations on substrings will also be familiar to the reader. Here epsilon (∈) is also a string, which represents nothing. It is empty string. In simpler terms a token can be called as a string. The operations on languages, which are not familiar to the reader, are discussed hereunder.

1. Kleene Closure

This to get zero or more concatenations and it is represented by *.

L^* → this will give zero or more concatenations of the language L.

Ex: a^* → will generate the following language

1. ∈
2. a
3. aa
4. aaa and
5. Others.

2. Positive Closure

This to get one or more concatenations, and it is represented by +.

L^+ → this will give one or more concatenations of the language L.

Ex: a^+ → will generate the following language

1. a
2. aa
3. aaa and
4. Others.

4.3.2 Regular Expressions (RE)

It is a special kind of notation used to define the language, which in turn defines the tokens or strings. The regular expressions are defined over the alphabet Σ. Σ is used to represent the character set and is also called alphabet.

If "*r*" is the regular expression and L (*r*) is the language denoted by that regular expression.

Examples of regular expressions:

(1) $(\text{digit})^+$ --- is regular expression for integer numbers, where
digit ⟶ 0 | 1 | 2 | ... | 9. And this is called regular definition. "|" represents the 'or' operator.

(2) letter (letter | digit) * — is the regular expression for variable names, where letter ⟶ A | .. | Z | a | .. | z.

(3) a* --- is the regular expression for generating zero or more no concatenations of a.

(4) ∈ is the regular expression for an empty string.

4.3.3 Finite Automata

These are language recognizers. Generally a recognizer will identify an entity, which is familiar to that, and say it is the same entity or it is not that entity. Similarly the automata will take the input token and say 'yes', if it is a sentence of the language and 'no', if it is not a sentence of the language.

The generalized transition diagram for a regular expression is called finite automata. It is a graph. It is a labeled, directed graph. Here the nodes are the states and the labeled edges are transitions.

The automata can be grouped into two as given below:

1. Non-deterministic Finite Automata (NFA)
2. Deterministic Finite Automata (DFA)

4.3.3.1 Non-Deterministic Finite Automata (NFA)

The automata, which satisfy the following conditions, can be called as Non-deterministic Automata.

1. These should have one start state
2. These should have one or more accepting or final states (generally these are double circled)
3. There can be ∈ transitions present and
4. There can be one or more transitions on a particular i/p symbol.

Example:

The NFA for the Regular expressions a*

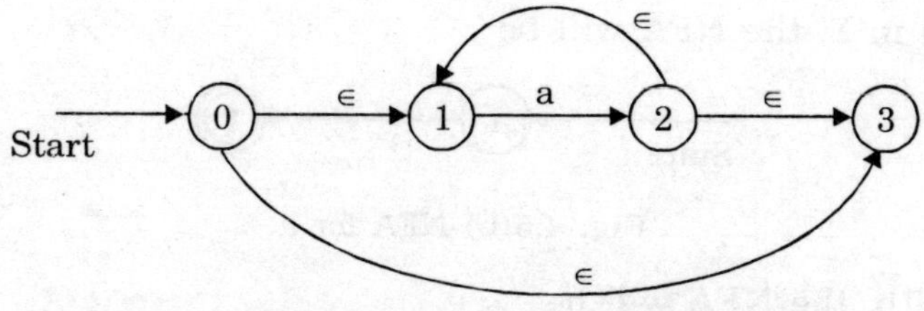

Fig. 4.3 NFA for the regular expression a*

The reader can understand from the above graph that "a" can appear zero instance or any number of instance in the language generated by the regular expression a*.

Deterministic Finite Automata (DFA)

The finite automata, which satisfy the following conditions, can be called as deterministic finite automata.

1. These should have one start state
2. These should have one or more accepting states
3. There cannot be '∈' transitions possible and
4. There can be only one transition possible on a particular i/p symbol.

Example: The DFA for the regular expression a*

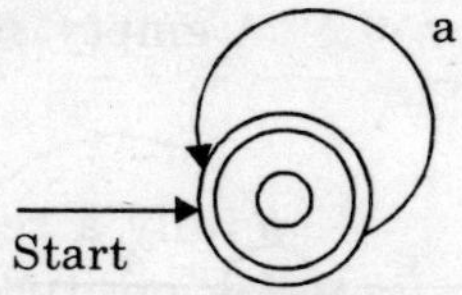

Fig. 4.4 DFA for the regular expression a*

For implementing the finite automata the following things must be done:

1. Conversion of RE to NFA
2. Conversion of NFA to DFA and
3. Minimize the DFA

We will discuss the above things in detail in the subsequent sections.

Conversion of RE into NFA

The steps involved are listed below:

Here the following notations are used:

i ⟶ initial state

f ⟶ final state

r ⟶ regular expression

N ⟶ NFA

1. For the RE, ∈, construct the NFA as

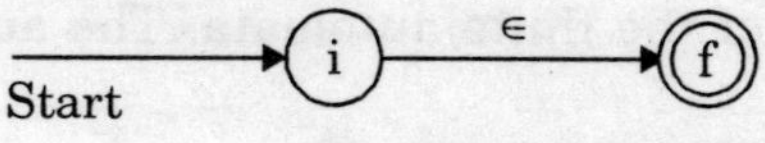

Fig. 4.5(a) NFA for ∈

2. For the RE a in Σ, the NFA will be

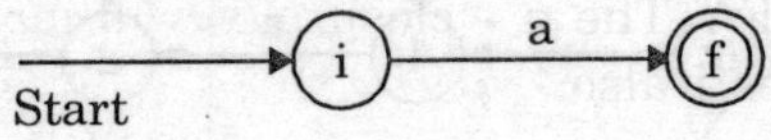

Fig. 4.5(b) NFA for a

3. For the RE a | b, the NFA will be

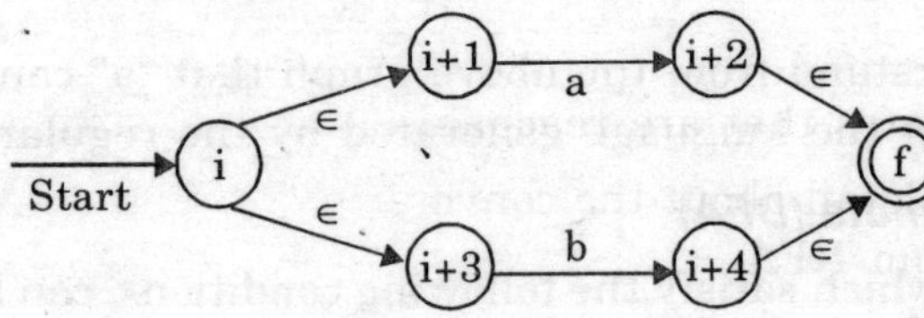

Fig. 4.5(c) NFA for a | b

4. For the RE ab, where a, b are two different regular expressions, the NFA will be

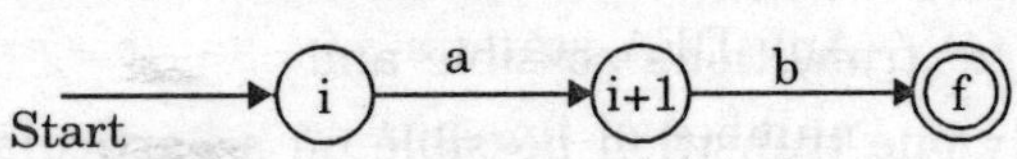

Fig. 4.5(d) NFA for I | ab

5. For RE a*

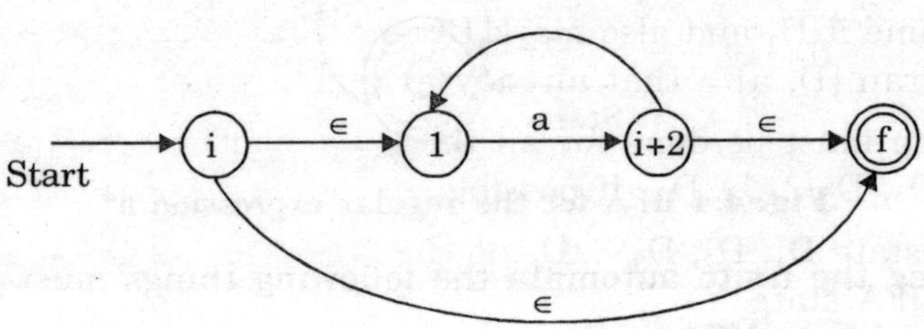

Fig. 4.5(e) NFA for a*

6. For any RE (R_1) the NFA will be same as that of NFA for R_1

Conversion of NFA Into DFA

This section discuss about the construction of DFA sets from the NFA. Before we discuss the construction of DFA sets, we will see following things.

1. Transition table
2. ∈ – Closure of a state i
3. ∈ – Closure of a set N
4. Move functions for a set N on an i/p symbol 'a'.

Transition Table

The finite automata can be conveniently represented in a table, called transition table. It is actually the tabular form of the finite automata. The automata may be either NFA or DFA.

$\in$ – Closure of an NFA state i

Consider any state i in an NFA. The $\in$ – closure (i) will include all the states which are reachable from i on $\in$. It includes i also.

$\in$ – Closure of N

(Here N is an NFA set)

This includes all the states that are reachable on $\in$ from any state i in the set N.

Move (N, a)

This includes all the states that are reachable from any state in N on a.

Now we can discuss in detail about the conversion of NFA into DFA. This involves the construction of DFA sets from NFA.

4.3.3.5 Steps for Construction of DFA Sets

Here i $\rightarrow$ initial state
N $\rightarrow$ Any NFA state
D $\rightarrow$ Any DFA state; a $\rightarrow$ an i/p symbol.
N $\rightarrow$ number of i/p symbols.

1. Find $\in$ - closure (i) and Name N and mark the state (marking is for identification) as the first DFA state D.
2. Find $\in$ - closure of Move (D, a) and check whether it is already marked DFA state, if not then Name it D_1 and also mark Dtran [D, a] = D_1. If it is already available then mark Dtran [D, a] = that already available state.
   (*a*) This step must be done for all the n i/p symbols for D and find the DFA states D_2, D_3, ...D_n if possible.
3. For any DFA state D_1, D_2, D_3 ....D_n do the step 2 for all the n i/p symbols till you find no new DFA state.

Dtran [D, a] represents the DFA transition of any DFA state D on the i/p symbol a.

Dtran [D, a] = D_1 means, the DFA state D reaches D_1 on a.

After doing the above steps the reader will be able to draw Dtran. This is nothing but the DFA - Transition table.

4.3.3.6 Steps for Minimization of DFA

This section discusses about the method for obtaining minimized DFA. This is called Min Dtran. This will result the DFA we are interested.

The collection of DFA states we have obtained will be considered, as input and the output will be minimized DFA states.

The collection of DFA states can be named as C.

Steps:

1. Divide C into two subgroups as C_S and C_F, where C_F will have the DFA states which are having accept or final states of NFA and C_S will be having the DFA states having non-final states of NFA.
2. Divide C_S and C_F using the following steps:

(a) Divide any group C such that two states S_1, S_2 are in the same group if S_1 and S_2 have same transitions for all the i/p symbols.

(b) Repeat step (a) for all the new subgroups obtained in step (a).

3. After partitioning into subgroups for C_S and C_F, representative from each group may be selected as follows.
4. Say (ABC) is a group and A, B, C has same transitions on all i/p symbols then A may be selected as representative and A will replace all the B, C occurrences.
5. The dead state may be removed. A state is dead, if that state is not accepting any transitions, and has no transitions on all the i/p symbols.
6. Remove all the states that are not reachable from the start state.

4.4 CONTEXT FREE GRAMMARS (CFG)

The context free grammars are useful in specifying the syntactical structures of a programming language. It is also called Backus-Naur-Form (BNF) description. It can simply be called as grammar in the subsequent discussions.

A Grammar has four quantities namely

1. Terminal
2. Non-terminal
3. A Start symbol
4. Production rules.

Terminals

These are the symbols, which are used to make strings in any language. In simpler terms the tokens can be called as terminals. We can say that the terminals are making various syntactical constructs.

Example: while, do and others.

Generally the terminals are represented by lowercase letters in this book.

Non-Terminals

These are the symbols, which are used to specify the strings. We can also say that the non-terminals are specifying the terminals or tokens.

Example: E, T, F and others.

Generally the non-terminals represented by the uppercase letters in this book.

Start Symbol

One non-terminal in a grammar, is selected as a start symbol. It actually specifies the language. The other non-terminals of the grammars are used to define the set of strings.

Production Rule

These rules define the way in which the syntactical constructs may be built, from the terminals. Each production rule consists of non-terminal followed by a string of non-terminals and terminals. This can simply be called as a production also.

Example:

E ⟶ E+T

Terminals:

+

Non-terminals:

E, T

An example grammar for simple arithmetic expression is given below:

E ⟶ E*E

E ⟶ E/E

E ⟶ E+E

E ⟶ E–E

E ⟶ id

Here there are five productions.

Terminals:

*,/,+,–,id

Non-terminals:

E

Start Symbol:

E

Some possible expressions, which can be generated from the above grammar, are given below:

1. id+id
2. id*id+id

4.4.1 Derivations and Reductions

In this section we will discuss about derivations and reductions of the CFG.

The non-terminals can be expanded. We can also say that the non-terminal can derive certain certain tokens (*i.e*) the tokens can be derived from the non-terminals. These are called derivations. We can also say these are expansions of non-terminals.

On the other hand the terminals does not derive any string (These are terminators). But the terminals can be reduced to any non-terminal. These are called reductions.

We can understand the derivations and expansions by the following example:

Consider the following grammar:

E ⟶ E+E

E ⟶ E*E

E ⟶ id

The derivations of the grammar for the string "id+id*id" is given as follows:

E ⟶ <u>E+E</u> [Expansion by E--→E+E]

E ⟶ E+<u>E*E</u> [Expansion by E--→E*E]

E ⟶ id+E*E [Expansion by E--→id]

E ⟶ id+id*E [Expansion by E--→id]

E ⟶ id+id*id [Expansion by E--→id]

Similarly the string "id+id*id" can be reduced to the starting non-terminal "E".

"id+id*id"

E ⟶ id+id*E [reduction by E--→id]

E ⟶ id+E*E [reduction by E--→id]

E ⟶ E+E*E [reduction by E--→id]

E ⟶ E+E [reduction by E--→E*E]

E ⟶ E [reduction by E--→E+E]

4.4.2 Parse Trees

The graphical representation for derivations that filters out the choice regarding the replacement order. This representation is called the parse tree.

For example consider the following grammar :

E ⟶ E+E

E ⟶ E*E

E ⟶ id

The input string given is " id+id*id".

The derivation of the grammar for the i/p string is given as follows:

E ⟶ E+E [Expansion by E--→E+E]

E ⟶ E+E*E [Expansion by E--→E*E]

E ⟶ id+E*E [Expansion by E--→id]

E ⟶ id+id*E [Expansion by E--→id]

E ⟶ id+id*id [Expansion by E--→id]

The above derivation can be graphically represented by the a tree as follows:

This tree is called the parse tree.

4.4.3 Ambiguous Grammar

If a Grammar produces more than one parse tree for the given input string, then in can be called as ambiguous grammar. Both the parse trees are drawn for any i/p string for a particular CFG. This i/p string cannot be parsed by certain type of parsers, because of its ambiguous nature. It is advisable that the ambiguity must be eliminated before parsing. Disambiguating rules can eliminate the ambiguity.

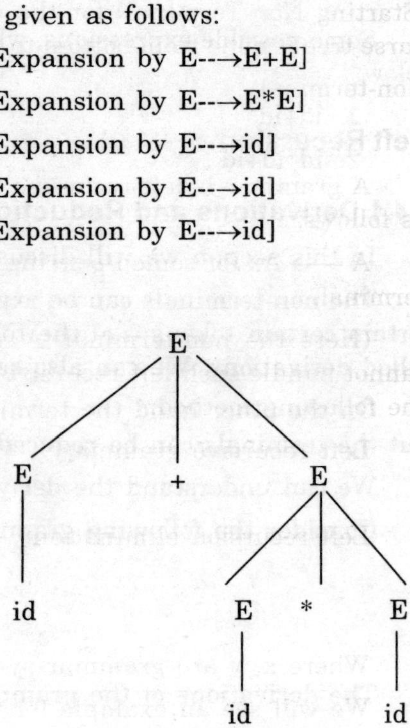

Fig. 4.6 Parse tree

4.5 SYNTAX ANALYZER

This receives valid tokens from the scanner and checks them against the grammar and produces the valid syntactical constructs. This is also called parser.

Parsers

Parser is a program, which receives valid tokens and checks them against the grammar and produces valid parse trees otherwise generates syntactical errors. It can be said that the parser generates valid syntactical constructs as per the grammar of the source language, from the valid tokens received from the lexical analyzer, and generates syntax errors otherwise.

Parsers can be classified into two broad categories namely,

1. Top Down parsers
2. Bottom Up parsers.

Top-Down Parsers

These are the parsers, which constructs the parse tree from the root (Starting Non-Terminal) to the leaves in preorder for the given i/p string. In simpler terms construction of the parse tree is done from top to bottom of the tree. Here the starting non-terminal is expanded to derive the given i/p string.

Botom up Parsers

These are the parsers, which constructs the parse tree from the leaves to the root (Starting Non-Terminal) for the given i/p string. In simpler terms the construction of the parse tree is done from bottom to top of the tree. Here the i/p string is reduced to the staring Non-terminal.

Left Recursion

A grammar is left recursive if it has a non-terminal A such that, there is a derivation as follows.

A ⟶ Ax for some i/p string, where x is a grammar symbol, either a terminal or a non-terminal.

(Here the non-terminal 'A' can be recursively called in the left). Top-down parsers cannot handle such left recursive grammars. This must be eliminated. This can be done by the following method.

Left recursive grammar:

$$A \longrightarrow Ax \mid y$$

Left recursion elimination:

$$A \longrightarrow yA'$$

$$A' \longrightarrow xA' \mid \epsilon$$

Where x, y are grammar symbols and ∈ is epsilon.

We will see an example for the above:

Left recursive grammar:

$$E \longrightarrow E+T \mid T$$

Apply the above rule :

Here A is E; x is +T; y is T;

So after left recursion elimination:

$$E' \longrightarrow TE'$$

$$E' \longrightarrow +TE' \mid \in$$

Left Factoring

This another useful transformation to make certain grammar suitable for parsing (Predictive). If a non-terminal has two choices for expansion which are same, then there will be confusion for selection of the choice, for a particular i/p string.

For example:

$$A \longrightarrow xB \mid xC$$

Now, there is a confusion which is to be selected for the any i/p string starting with x. This problem can be solved by left factoring.

Left factoring is a transformation for factoring out the common prefixes. For the above grammar the application of left factoring will result as

$$A \longrightarrow xA'$$

$$A' \longrightarrow B \mid C$$

4.5.1 Non-Recursive Predictive Parser

It is a top-down parser. As name implies it is not recursive. This needs the following components to check whether the given string is successfully parsed or not.

1. I/P Buffer
2. Stack
3. Parsing routine and parsing table

The input buffer is keeping the input string to be parsed. The input string is followed by a symbol '$'. This is used to indicate that the input string is terminated. This is used as right end marker.

The stack is keeping always the grammar symbols. The grammar symbols will be either non-terminals or terminals. Initially the stack is pushed with "$" on the top of the stack. After that, as parsing progresses the grammar symbols are pushed. This '$' is used to announce the completion of parsing.

The parsing table is generally a two dimensional array. An entry in the table is referred T[A, a], where 'A' is a nonterminal 'a', is a terminal and T is table name.

The parsing routine works in conjunction with the parsing table. This is a program which can be written in languages like C, C++ and Java. The parsing program reads from i/p buffer and considers the symbol on the top of the stack, and works in conjunction with parsing table T, and announces the o/p as successfully parsed or not.

Steps involved in Non recursive predictive parsing

1. I/P buffer is filled with i/p string with $ as the right end marker.
2. Stack is initially pushed with $.
3. Construction of parsing table T.

3.1 For construction of T, FIRST and FOLLOW of the grammar symbols have to be computed.

4. Parsing by parsing routine.

We will first see the computation of FIRST and FOLLOW functions, since these are very much necessary in constructing the parsing table T.

4.5.2 Computation of First

(Here we keep X, Y, Z as grammar symbols. The grammar symbol may represent either a non-terminal or a terminal)

FIRST function determines, the beginning terminals which are derived from particular grammar symbol.

Steps involved in computation of FIRST

1. If X is a terminal, then FIRST (X) is X itself

   For example, FIRST (id)=> {id}

2. If X is a non-terminal, then FIRST(X) is set of terminals derived from X.

   For example, FIRST(F) and F-> (E)

   So FIRST (F)=> {(}

   2.1 If X-> ∈, then FIRST (X) will have ∈ as its FIRST.

3. Consider a production

   X -> YZ

   Y -> ∈

   Z -> a

   Here FIRST (Z) => {a}

   FIRST (Y) => {∈}

   As per above steps

   FIRST (X) => {∈}

   This can be done for all productions which satisfy the above conditions.

4. If there is a production X -> Y then FIRST (X) = FIRST (Y).

   For example, We will compute FIRST for the following grammar

   G: S -> (L) | a

   L -> SL′

   L′ ->, SL′ | ∈

The above grammar can be written as

S -> (L)

S -> a

L -> SL′

L′ ->, SL′

L′ -> ∈

By using the steps, the FIRST can be computed as follows

FIRST (S) => {(,a}

FIRST (L) => FIRST (S)

⇒ {(,a}

FIRST (L′) => {,,∈}

4.5.3 Computation of Follow

FOLLOW determines the set of terminals which can appear immediately after a grammar symbol. FOLLOW in simpler words, set of terminals which follow the particular grammar symbol.

Steps involved in computation of FOLLOW

1. If S is a starting non-terminal, then FOLLOW (S) will have "$" in its FOLLOW

   For example, FOLLOW (S) => {$}; S is a start symbol.

2. If A => XBY

Where A, B are non-terminals and X, Y are grammar symbols, which may be either terminals of non-terminals.

Then FOLLOW (B) => FIRST (Y) except ∈

Example:

L′ -> ,SL′

As per the above step

∴ FOLLOW (S) => {$,,}

Since FIRST (L′) = {,∈} as discussed in the above section.

3. If A -> XB (or)

A -> XBY and FIRST (Y) has ∈, Then

Whatever in FOLLOW (A) will be in FOLLOW (B).

Example:

L -> SL′ and

L′ -> ,SL′ (consider this one alone not L′ -> ∈)

∴ FOLLOW (L′) will have the terminals available in FOLLOW (L)

Suppose FOLLOW (L) = {,}

Then FOLLOW (L′) = {,}

4.5.4 Construction of Parsing Table (T)

As discussed already it is generally a two dimensional array. It has rows as non-terminals and columns as terminals, the symbol '$' is used as the last column. The parsing routine works in conjunction with this table T.

Steps involved in construction of parsing table (T)

1. If there is a production A -> X then do the following steps.

   1.1 For each terminal 'a' in FIRST (X), add A -> X to T [A, a] (X is a grammar symbol).

1.2 If FIRST (X) has ∈, then for each terminal 'b' in FOLLOW (A), add A -> X to T [A, b]

1.3 If FIRST (X) has ∈ and '$' is in FOLLOW (A), then add A -> X to T [A, $]

2. Make all the undefined entries as errors.

4.5.5 Parsing Algorithm

This algorithm works in conjunction with parsing table T. Here the stack keeps the grammar symbols and the i/p Buffer keeps the input string with '$' as the right end marker.

Let us say 'TOP' represents the grammar symbol on the top of the stack and 'p' represents input symbol from the i/p buffer. Steps for parsing:

1. If TOP = p = $, the parser completes parsing and announce successful completion ('TOP' is here terminal).
2. If TOP = p ≠ $, then the parser pops 'TOP' off the stack and advances the i/p pointer to the next i/p symbol, (here 'TOP' is a terminal).
3. If TOP is a nonterminal, then parser consults the entry T [TOP, p] in the table T. If T [TOP, p] is a production A -> XYZ then parser pushes the ZYX on the stack by replacing the TOP [here TOP = A].
4. If T [TOP, p] = error, then the parser calls an error recovery routine or generates error messages.

4.6 LR PARSERS

These kinds of parsers are Bottom-up parsers. These are efficient parsers. The expansions for L and R are as follows:

L -> Left to right

R -> Right most derivation

The name is used because, these parsers scan the i/p from left to right and construct a rightmost derivation (parse tree) in reverse.

LR parsers generally have two major components as given below:

1. Parsing algorithm
2. Parsing table

As discussed in the previous sections the parsing algorithm works in conjunction with the parsing table. The algorithm and construction of parsing table are different from other parsers.

Apart from the above two components an i/p buffer is used to keep the i/p string. A stack is also used in this parser, to keep the grammar symbols and states. The states will be discussed later.

There are three ways to construct the LR parsing tables as listed below:

1. SLR (Simple LR)
2. CLR (Canonical LR) and,
3. LALR (Look Ahead LR)

We will see each parser in detail in the subsequent sections.

The parsing algorithm is common for all the three cases. The parsing tables are different for each case. We will discuss about construction of SLR parsing table and then LR parsing algorithm (which is common for all), and also some examples.

4.6.1 SLR Parser

In order to construct the SLR parsing table the following two components are necessary.

1. Construction of sets of LR (0) items collection using CLOSURE function and goto function.
2. Construction of parsing table using LR (0) items

Let us discuss the above in detail hereunder.

4.6.1.1 Construction of LR (0) items collection

The collection of sets of LR (0) items is called 'C'. This must be constructed in order to construct SLR parsing table. The collection of sets of LR (0) items can be constructed with the help of functions called CLOSURE and goto. This collection is called canonical collection of LR (0) items.

LR (0) item:

Let us first define what an LR (O) item here is,

Consider a production I -> JKL in grammar G.

Now place a ('.') at some position at the right side of the production as shown below:

I -> •JKL

I -> J•KL

I -> JK•L

I -> JKL•.

These are called LR (0) items of the grammar G.

LR (0) item of a grammar G, is a production of G with a dot at some position of the right side. LR (0) item can be simply called as an item also.

Example:

E -> id is the production; the LR (0) items are :

E -> •id

E -> id•

If there is an epsilon production like I -> ∊, then I -> • is the item.

We will discuss augmented grammar and CLOSURE function, GOTO function because these are necessary for construction of collection of LR (0) items.

4.6.2 Augmented Grammar

Consider the grammar G and S is the start symbol. The augmented grammar of G is G' with a new start symbol S′ and having a production S′ -> S.

Example:

Consider the grammar G

S -> AS

S -> b

A -> SA

A -> a

The augmented grammar G′

S' -> S

S -> b

A -> SA

A -> a

4.6.3 The CLOSURE Function

Let us say I is a set of items for a grammar G, then closure of I (CLOSURE (I)) can be computed by using the following steps:

1. Initially, every item in I is added to Closure (I)
2. Consider the following:

A -> X•BY - an item in I

B -> Z - a production

Then add the item B -> Z to I, if it is not already there.

This rule has to be applied till no new items can be added to Closure (I)

(**Note:** X, Y, Z are grammar symbols)

Example:

Consider the item in I

S -> A•S

Closure (I) => Closure (S -> A•S)

S -> •AS

S -> •b

Here we have to include the items derived from A also

∴ A -> •SA

A -> •a

The items derived from S are already there. So there can be no new items, included to I.

Closure (I):

S -> A•S

S -> •AS

S -> •b

A -> •SA

A -> •a

4.6.4 GOTO Function

This is computed for a set I on a grammar symbol X. What is the set I reaches on X or does it create a new set on X, can be computed by the function GOTO (I, X).

Consider an item in I

A -> •XBY then

Goto (I, X) will be

$\Rightarrow$ A -> X •BY including the closure of B.

X is a grammar symbol.

Example:

Consider I:
S -> A •.S
S -> •AS
S -> •b
A -> •SA
A -> •a

Then goto (I, S)
S -> AS•
A -> S •A
A -> •SA
A -> •a
S -> • AS
S -> •b

Similarly goto (I, b)
S -> b•

(**Note:** check for the grammar symbol X, preceded by • and if X is a nonterminal include its closure after advancing the •, and if X is a terminal advance the • alone).

Now we will compute the LR (0) items collection for a grammar. This is also called canonical collection of LR (0) items.

4.6.5 SLR Parsing Table Construction

This parsing table is also a two dimensional array in which the rows are states and columns are terminals and non-terminals. This table has two parts as

1. Action entries
2. Goto entries

The action may be any one of the following:

1. Shift
2. Reduce
3. Accept and
4. Error

The goto entries will be having state numbers like 1, 2, 3 etc.

State

Consider a set I_j in the collection of LR (0) items. Here 'j' is the state, which is used in parsing the input string,

Example:

I_0 ; 0 is the state.

The goto entries indicate the transition of a state 'i' to 'j' on a particular nonterminal.

Now let us discuss the steps involved construction of SLR parsing table.

4.6.6 Steps for Constructing SLR Parsing Table

1. Let C = {I_0, I_1, ..I_n} collection of sets of LR (0) items
2. Consider Ij as a set in C

   2.1 If goto (I_j, a) = I_k then set action [j, a] to "shift K" and 'a' is always terminal.

Example:

Goto (I_0, id) = I_5

Set the action [0, id] = shift 5

2.2 If A-> X., (X can be either terminal or a non terminal) is In I_j then

2.3 Set action [j, a] to "reduce A -> X" for all "a" in FOLLOW (A) if X is a terminal, if X is a non terminal set action [j, a] to "reduce A -> X" for all 'a' in FOLLOW (X).

Example:

I_5: F -> id•

and FOLLOW (F) = {+, *,), $}

Action [5, +], action [5, *]

Action [5,)], action [5, $] will have the entries "reduce F -> id".

Note: Here 'A' should not be S'.

3. If [S' -> S•] is in I_j then set action [j, $] to "accept"
4. If goto (I_j, A) = I_k then set goto [j, A] = K
5. All the undefined entries are errors.

4.6.7 SLR Parsing

This algorithm works in conjunction with the parsing table, for parsing an i/p string. The possible parsing actions are as follows:

1. Shift
2. Reduce by a production
3. Accept and halt
4. Error

The i/p string is in i/p buffer followed by the right end marker $. The stack keeps the states of the parsing table.

The i/p strings has n symbols and are marked by $a_1a_2........a_n$, and the stack has states $S_0S_1S_m$.

Algorithm for SLR Parsing

1. If action [S_o, a_1] = S_j, the parser has to make a shift of the current i/p symbol, and new state will be 'j' on the stack.

   For example:

   $s_o = 0$

$a_1 = id$

Action [0, id] = S_5, the parser has to shift the terminal 'id', 5 will be new state on the stack. Now the stack will have "oid5".

2. If Action [S_m, a_i] = reduce by A -> X, and then the parser has to reduce by

A -> X.

Find out the number of symbols available on the right hand side of A after ->, Let us say it r. Then pop off 2.r symbols from the stack.

2.1 If goto [S_{m-r}, A] = J (state) then push 'A, J' on to the stack.

Example:

Action [5, *] = r6 (6th production)

Here we must reduce by F -> id, suppose the stack contents are 0id5,

Here $r = 1$

$2r = 2$

Pop 2 symbols off the stack, so the stack will have 0.

Goto [S_{m-r}, A] = Goto [0, F] = 3

Then push F, 3 on to the stack.

Now the new contents of stack will be 'OF3'.

3. If Action [S_m, a_i] = accept, then announce that the parsing is completed successfully, and then halt.
4. If Action [S_m, a_i] = error, then the parser encounters error and calls error recovery routine or generates error message.

4.7 SYNTAX DIRECTED TRANSLATIONS

SDT is a notational frame work, of the valid syntactical constructs received from the syntax analyzer, to make it suitable for intermediate code generation. This attaches actions or rules or subroutines of the grammar.

4.7.1 Attributes

The properties of an entity are called the attributes. The attributes may be the address, value, scope, type and others. Here we discuss about the attributes of the production rule of the grammars. There are two kinds of attributes namely.

1. Synthesized attributes and
2. Inherited attributes.

Synthesized Attributes

If the attributes of the parent depend on the attributes of the children then such attributes are called synthesized attributes.

Inherited Attributes

If the attributes of the children depend on the attributes of the parents then such attributes are called inherited attributes. The children generally inherit the properties of the parent.

4.7.2 Syntax Directed Translation

This is a special kind of notation used to attach the semantic actions to the production rules of the grammar. The semantic action is called semantic rule or output action. The semantic action may be invoking subroutine, a computation and the like.

TRANSLATION is nothing but associating a value to a grammar symbol.

The syntax directed translation could be of two types:

1. Synthesized translation
2. Inherited translation

Before we see further we will see some examples for the attributes, which will help in discussing the above two translations.

Consider the grammar:

$$S \longrightarrow AS$$
$$S \longrightarrow b$$
$$A \longrightarrow SA$$
$$A \longrightarrow a$$

Let us draw a parse tree for the string

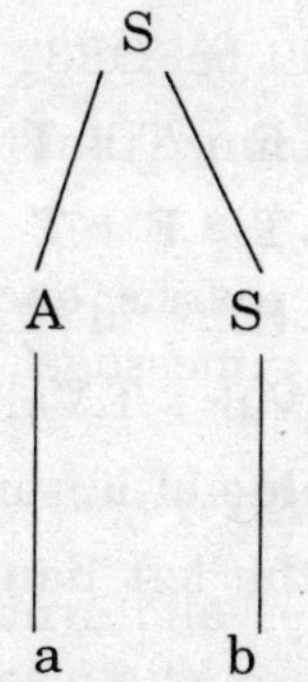

Fig. 4.7 Synthesized attribute

Here S is the parent of A, b and A is the parent of a. The attribute type of S, depends on the types of its children, such attributes are synthesized attributes.

Example:

{S.type : = b.type}

Note: (SDTs are given within set brackets)

Consider the Grammar

$E_a \longrightarrow E_b + E_c$

$E_a \longrightarrow id$

The value of E_a will be depending on the values of E_b and E_c.

{E_a.val : = E_b.val + E_c.val}

{E_a.val : = value (id)}

Consider an example as shown below

$$A \longrightarrow X$$

The parse tree

A is the parent.

Fig. 4.8 Inherited attribute

Suppose value X is depending on the value of A, then such attributes are called inherited attributes.

Example:

{X.val : = 3 * A.val}

4.7.3 Synthesized Translation

If the translation of the parent depends on the translations of the children, then such a translation is called synthesized translation. Here attributes of the parent depend on the attributes of the children.

Consider the grammar:

$$E \longrightarrow E + T \mid T$$

$$T \longrightarrow T * F \mid T$$

$$F \longrightarrow (E) \mid id$$

{E.Val : = E.Val + T.Val}

{F.val : = value of id} are synthesized translations.

We can also say that translation on the left hand side symbol is depending on the translations of the right hand side symbols.

4.7.4 Inherited Translation

If the translation of the children is depending on the translation of the parent, then such translation can be called as **inherited translation.** Here the attributes of the children are depending on the attributes of the parent. (inherits the properties).

Example:

Consider the production

$$A \longrightarrow X$$

{X.val : = A.val} is an inherited translation.

We can also say that the translation on the right hand side symbol depends on the translation of the left hand side symbol.

4.8 INTERMEDIATE CODE GENERATION

The Intermediate code generator receives syntax directed translated syntactical constructs and represent them in any one of the following intermediate codes

1. Postfix
2. Syntax tree, and
3. Three address code.

4.8.1 Postfix

The reader is probably familiar with postfix notations. This is also one type of Intermediate code representation. It is also called reverse polish notation.

We will see an example:

Consider an i/p string "a+b" (This is called infix expression).

The postfix expression is "ab+".

The reader can refer any data structure book for more details. This type of intermediate code representation is not now generally used in the compilers.

4.8.2 Syntax Trees

It is a type of intermediate code representation, which is very similar to parse tree. It is an abstract tree, which removes the redundant information from the parse tree.

The syntax tree for the i/p string "a+b" is given below:

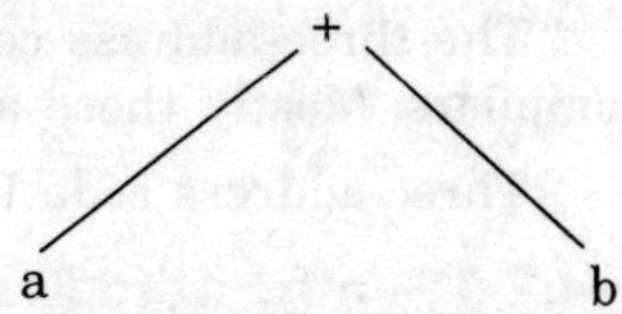

Fig. 4.9 Syntax tree for "a+b"

We will see another example. Consider the i/p string "id*id+id".

The syntax tree is given below:

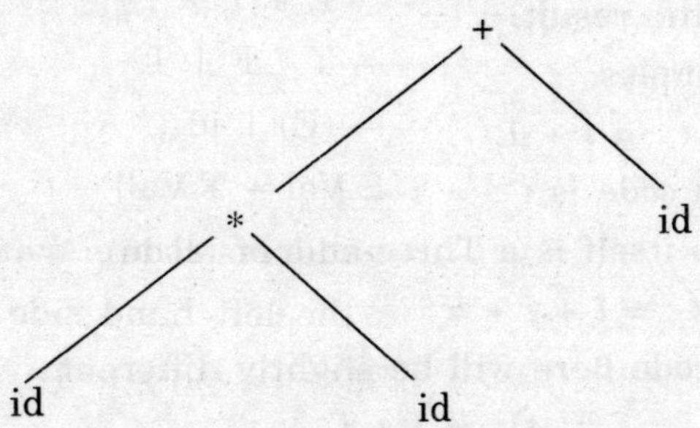

Fig. 4.10 Syntax tree for "id*id+id"

The corresponding parse tree is also given below:

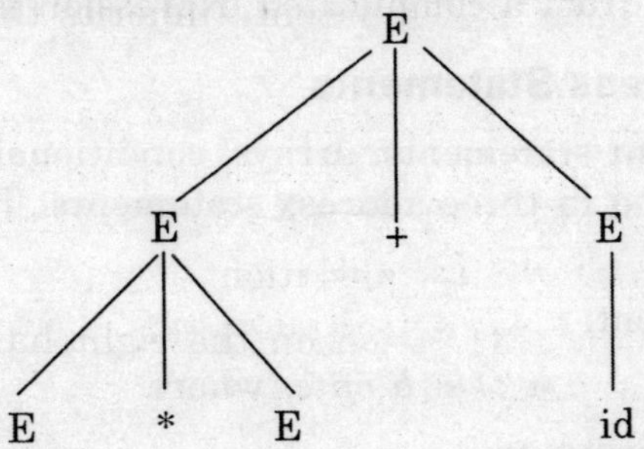

Fig. 4.11 Parse tree for "id*id+id"

Now the reader can understand the concepts of parse trees and syntax trees. The comparisons are listed below:

1. The syntax trees will have operators as roots but the parse trees will have the non-terminals as their roots.
2. A CFG is essential for drawing a parse tree, but for syntax tree an expression is essential (i/p string).

This type of intermediate code representation is not also widely used in the compilers.

Directed Acyclic Graph (DAG) is special kind of tree used in optimizing compilers, which slightly varies form syntax trees.

4.8.3 Three Address Codes

The three-address code is a type of intermediates code, which are popularly used in compilers. Mostly these are helpful in optimizing compilers.

Three-address code is sequence of statements of the general form as given below:

$$a := b\ op\ c$$

Where a, b and c are identifier names, constants, or compiler generated temporary variable names, and "*op*" represents operator, which may be any binary operator, like arithmetic operator, or relational operator, or a boolean operator. And the symbol ":=" stands for assignment operator.

This representation is called three-address code because it has three-addresses, two for the operands and one for the result.

We will see some examples.

1. The expression is $i := i + 1$.

   The three-address code is $i := i + 1$

   (Here the expression itself is a Three-address code).

2. The expression is $i := i + j + k$

   The three-address code here will be slightly different.

$$t1 := i + j$$

$$i := t1 + k,$$

Where $t1$ is compiler-generated temporary variable name. The method making a sequence of three-address statements, from a complicated expression is called unraveling.

4.8.4 Types of Three-Address Statements

Segments like assignment statements, arrays, conditional statements, procedure calls, and others can be represented in three-address statements. There are few examples given hereunder.

1. Assignment statement:

   The general form : $a := b\ op\ c$, where

   "*op*" is any binary operator.

   Example: $i := i + 1$

2. Assignment statement:

   The general form : $a := op\ c$, where

"*op*" is any unary operator.

Example : $i := -1$

(**Note:** If an operator, operates on two operands then it can be called as a binary operator.

Example: +,*,–, in the expressions $a+b$, $i*j$, $k–l$.

If an operator, operates on only one operand then it can be called as an unary operator.

Example: !, –, in the expressions $a!$, –b etc.! is logical negation operator).

3. Copy statements of the form $a := b$, where b is copied or assigned to a.
4. Unconditional goto statements like goto *xx*, where *xx* is a label.
5. Conditional branching statements like "if a OP *b* goto *xx*", where OP is any relational operator and *a*, *b* are operands.
6. Procedure call statements like "add (*a*, *b*)" and return statements like "return sum" are also three address statements only.
7. Assignment statements in arrays like "$a[i] = x$ and $x[i] = a$".
8. Assignment statements using pointers like "$a = \&b$ and $b = *a$" are also three address statements.

4.8.5 Quadruples, Triples and Indirect Triples

The three-address codes are generally implemented using any one of the following representations.

1. Quadruples
2. Triple and
3. Indirect triples.

We will see here how these representations are used to implement the three-address codes considering an example.

4.8.6 Quadruples

Quadruple is a record structure used to represent three-address codes, with four fields (quad means four) as listed below:

1. op
2. arg1
3. arg2 and
4. Result.

(**Note:**

op — operator

arg1 — argument1

arg2 — argument2)

Now we will see an example.

Example:

The expression is $i := i + j + k$

The three-address codes are

$t1 := i + j$

$i := t1 + k$, where $t1$ is a temporary variable.

The quadruple representations are given in the following Fig. 4.12.

	OP	Arg 1	Arg2	Result
(0)	+	i	j	t_1
(1)	+	T_1	K	i

Fig. 4.12 Quadruple representation

4.8.7 Triples

Triple is also a record structure used to represent the three-address codes, which has only three fields as listed below:

1. op
2. arg1 and
3. arg2.

This record structure eliminates the temporary variables and instead these are referred by their corresponding position (pointers).

The triple representations are Fig. 4.13.

	OP	Arg 1	Arg2
(0)	+	i	i
(1)	+	(0)	K

Fig. 4.13 Triple representation

4.8.8 Indirect Triples

This is another implementation of three-address code, which lists pointers to triples than listing the triples themselves. This is called indirect triples.

The indirect triple representations are Fig. 4.14.

	Pointers to Input
(0)	111
(1)	112

	OP	Arg 1	Arg2
(0)	+	i	i
(1)	+	(0)	K

Figure 4.14 Indirect triple representation

4.9 SYMBOL TABLE AND ERRORS

In this section we will see the common phases to the other phases of the compiler called symbol table and error handler. Each phase of the compiler consults symbol table and also error handler whenever necessary. We will first discuss the symbol table. The symbol table management is also called as book keeping.

4.9.1 Symbol Tables

The symbol table keeps track of scope, binding information and other attributes of the symbols. The symbol may be a name of an identifier and the like program segments. The attributes of the symbols are maintained in the symbol table. There will be entries in the symbol table for any name in the source program. The attributes like scope, binding information will vary as the program is being executed. So the symbol table has to be maintained dynamically. There will be new entries of any name during the run-time. If the size of symbol table is to be allotted statically, it should foresee the changes in the symbol table entries and accordingly the size has to be allocated. Sometimes there will be new names also have to be added.

The symbol table entries are names and their attributes only. In a programming language there will be some keywords or reserved words, and names of the programming segments like variables should not have such names. So the symbol tables should have reserved words or key words so as to check the names from the source program when encountered.

The source program sometimes have the same name assigned to two different program segments, for example the 'diff' is the name of a (scalar) variable; and the same name may be available variable for an array too; 'sco' may be a local variable of function fun1 and it will also another local variable of a function say fun2. So the symbol table must have to separate those things into different entities. There can be a separate entry for each entity.

The names can be stored in the symbol table using fixed sized arrays or dynamically using pointers.

The data structures for symbol tables can be

1. Linear list and
2. Hash tables.

The readers can refer for more details in the assemblers (Chapter 5), topic symbol table management (5.8).

4.9.2 Errors

Error handler is one of the phases of compiler. All the other phases of the compiler consults the error handler phase when errors are encountered during compilation of a program. The compiler must detect the errors and should report the errors to the user in understandable format.

4.10 CODE OPTIMIZATION

The code (here code refers to the intermediate code and mostly three-address code) optimizer receives intermediate codes and optimize them considering the factors like memory, execution time and others. This phase removes the redundant codes. It is an optional phase. The compiler, which has code optimization phase is called optimizing compilers.

Code optimization is the process of modifying the working code to a more optimal code based on a particular goal. The optimizations are generally done on a working code.

The process of making optimal code is rarely possible because optimization of code with respect to all the factors like memory, execution time and others will not be possible. If the code is occupying less space then its execution time will be more. If it is having less execution time then it is more complex. So the optimal code is generally not possible. But we can say the code is comparatively improved. Improved code is the right word than the optimal code. So the optimization techniques can better be called as code improving transformations.

4.10.1 Necessity of Code Optimization

In the programs having loops, there something called 90–10 rule. This rule tells that 90% of the execution time is spent only in the 10% of code. In loops some loop invariant computations are generally present. If these loop independent computations, can be brought out of the loop, the execution time will be reduced. This gives scope for optimization of the code. This is an example for the possibility of the optimization. There are similar things available which give more scope for optimization. Optimization depends on various factors like:

1. Memory and
2. Execution time

4.10.2 Code Improving Transformations

The code improvement can be possible by using the code improving transformations. These are generally called optimization techniques. Some of the codes improving transformations are discussed hereunder.

4.10.2.1 Constant Folding

This is actually compile time evaluation. This makes possible for the computations performed during the execution time itself, and thus avoids the computation during the execution time. Constant folding is nothing but replacing the runtime compilation by compile time computation.

Example:

a: = (22/7) * (r*r)

In the above example 22/7 can be computed during the compilation time itself than computing in each execution.

4.10.2.2 Constant Propagation

Propagation means propagating an entity from one statement to another statement. This is done for constants. We can understand this by an example.

Consider the following three address statements

```
temp1 = 4;
...
....
temp2 = temp1 * 2;
```

Here the variable temp1 is propagated. This can be optimized as given below during the compile time itself.

```
temp1 = 4;
...
....
temp2 = 4 * 2;
```

This is actually constant propagation. Constant propagation is nothing but replacement of a variable by a constant that appears on the rhs of an assignment for that variable. This is done during the compile time. The variable should not be redefined along the path of its use.

4.10.2.3 Common Sub-expression Elimination (CSE)

This can be explained by the following example.

Consider following code:

```
a = x + y;
...
....
b = x + y + z;
```

The above can be optimized as follows:

```
temp3 = x + y;
a = temp3;
...
...
b = temp3 + z;
```

In the second case the computation is done for "x+y" only once. But in the previous case twice the computations are done; "x+y" is here common sub-expression. The common sub-expression elimination allows no recomputations of an expression which is evaluated already. The common sub-expression should not be redefined along the path of its use.

4.10.2.4 Variable Propagation or Copy Propagation

Copy propagation means the use of variable v1 in place of v2. Consider the following statements:

```
v1 = v2;
```

...

....

h = v1 + f;

g = v2 + f – 6;

In statement 2, v2 can be used in place of v1 by copy propagation. The transformed statements will be as listed below:

v1 = v2;

...

...

...

h = v2+f;

g = v2+f–6;

This leads for common sub-expression elimination further.

4.10.2.5 Dead Code Elimination

A variable is dead if not used subsequently *i.e.*, it is not live. The code is useless. This dead code may appear in the program generally accidentally. This dead code can be eliminated.

The above discussed transformations are said to be function preserving transformations.

4.10.3 Basic Blocks

The discussion of basic blocks will be much useful for discussing about loop optimizations in the subsequent sections. The basic block is a sequence of consecutive statements in which the flow of control enters at the beginning and leaves at the end without halt or possibility of branching except at the end.

Example:

```
temp1 = i+1;
temp2 = t1*2;
temp3 = temp1+ i;
```

A program will be generally represented into three-address statements by intermediate code generator. These must be divided into basic blocks. We will see how the three-address statements are represented into basic blocks.

4.10.3.1 Steps for Partition of Three-Address Statements into Basic Blocks

1. Determine the leader by using the following rules:
   - 1.1 The first statement is a leader.
   - 1.2 Any statement that is the target of a conditional or unconditional goto statement is a leader.
   - 1.3 Any statement that immediately follows a goto or unconditional goto statement is a leader.
2. For each leader, its basic block consists of the leader and all the statements upto not including the next leader or the end of the program.

4.10.4 Flow Graphs

The basic blocks can be represented graphically with flow-of-control information is called a flow graph. It is directed graph. The nodes are basic blocks in flow graph. One node is marked as initial. This node must have leader as the first statement. There is a directed edge from block B1 to B2 if B2 immediately follows B1 in some execution sequence.

This can be found if the following conditions are satisfied.

1. If there is a conditional or unconditional jump from the last statement of B1 to the first statement of B2.

Or

2. If B2 immediately follows B1 in the order of program, B1 does not end in an unconditional jump.

Here B1 is a predecessor of B2, and B2 is successor of B1.

4.10.5 Loops

Loop is a collection of nodes in a flow graph, which much satisfy the following conditions.

1. All the nodes in the collection must be strongly connected, i.e from any node in the loop to any other, there should be a path of length of length one or more, wholly within the loop.
2. The collection of nodes should have unique entry.

The loop, which contains any other loop can be called as an inner loop.

4.10.6 Loop Optimizations

In this section we will see the optimization techniques for loops. Loop optimization is very important since it gives more improvement.

We will see mainly the following optimization techniques:

1. Code motion or loop invariant computation.
2. Induction variable elimination and
3. Reduction in strength.

Code Motion or Loop Invariant Computation

The computations which are independent of execution of loop parameters, and are present inside the loop can be brought before the loop. These are loop invariant computations.

Induction variable Elimination

Any two variables are said to be induction variables if there is a change in any one of the variable, then there will be corresponding change in the other variable. The variables x, y are said to be induction variables, if x is incremented then y will also be correspondingly incremented or decremented. These induction variables give scope for optimization *i.e.*, it allows to use only one variable instead of using both.

Reduction in strength

Replacing the costly operator by cheap operator is called reduction in strength.

Example:

t1 = a**2;

This can be transformed as t1 = a*a;

Here the costly operator ** is replaced *, comparatively a cheap operator.

The reader can find many examples for this optimization technique.

4.11. Code Generation

It is the last phase of the compiler. This phase receives optimized inter mediate code, generates the code for execution. The code generated generally will be relocatable machine code or assembly code.

The last phase of the compiler is to generate the executable code. This phase generally receives the input from the intermediate code generator from non-optimizing compilers or from the code optimizer in case of optimizing compilers.

The i/p to the code generator must be error free. It must have undergone, lexical analysis, syntax analysis, semantic analysis phases, and also free from the respective errors.

The target program may be

1. assembly language
2. relocatable machine code or
3. Absolute machine language

The absolute machine language code is ready to be executed, and stored in fixed location in memory. The relocatable machine code can be linked by linker and loaded by loader for execution. The assembly language will have codes in symbolic instructions, for the given source program. The assembler will generate the code to be executed, from the assembly code (symbolic code).

4.11.1 Architecture of Machine for Code Generation

The architecture of the machine affects the codes be generated. The instruction set of the machine also does affect the code generation. This can be understood by the following example:

Consider the three-address code:

i = i + 1;

If the instruction 'INC' available, then it can be implemented easily by INC. If it is not available then the following steps to be done.

1. i must be loaded to a register R
2. Then the contents of register (R) must be incremented by one
3. Then the contents of register (R) must be loaded into I

The above steps can be done for in an assembly language program. So instruction set is important for code generation, and also the selection of instructions for implementing the three-address codes. The availability of registers also affects the code generation. Better utilization of registers for code generation is also to be considered. Register referenced instructions are faster than the memory referenced instructions. Some instructions will make use of register pairs for operands and results. The computation order is also to be considered for the generation of code. The readers can assume any standard m/c and its instruction set and other addressing modes, for the target machine, for which the codes are to be generated.

4.11.2 Instruction costs

The cost of an instruction corresponds to the length of the instruction. The instructions, which use registers, have minimal cost. The cost refers to the length of the instruction. The length correspond the number of words (in turn operands) in the instructions, so it affects the time taken to refer the operands and ultimately the execution time. If the instruction cost is reduced, it will lead to minimization of time for executing the instruction. So this factor also to be considered for code generation.

We will see some instructions and their costs

Table 4.1 Instruction costs

Instruction	Cost
MOV R0, R1	1 (It uses one word transfer)
MOV R0, M	2 (It has two words transfer; M-memory)
ADD 02, R3	2 (R3-one word; 02→ one word)

4.11.3 Code Generation

In this section we will see how codes are actually generated? And what are the other issues to be considered in code generation? It is quite clear that this code generation receives three-address codes as input. Before discussing about code generation algorithm we will see some necessary things for code generation.

Next-Use Information

The statements (three-address codes) will be used in the subsequent basic blocks in a flow graph or a name in a statement will be used by some other statement. So we can understand that a name or statement will be used again (next-use) in a program.

Consider the following diagram.

Here the names a, b in B1 are used in the statements a1, b1 in B2. Now we will define the next use information.

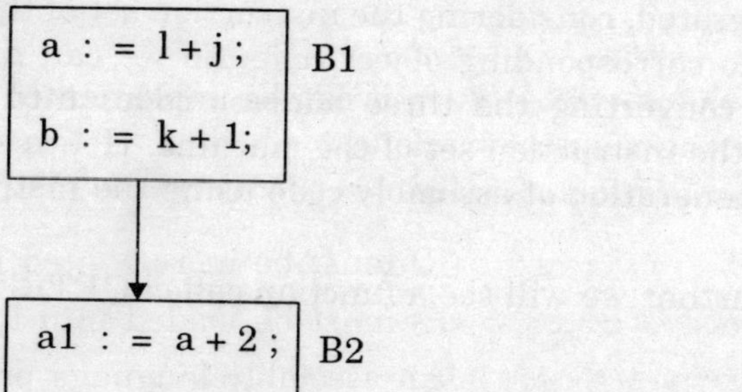

Fig. 4.15. Next use of name

Next-use Information

If a statement or a name in a statement is used in another statement, then that statement or that name is said to be next-used, and in between, the statement or name should not redefined (reassigned). This information can be called as next-use information.

If the name is used by another statement then the name is said to be live. If any other statement does not use it then the name is not live or dead.

From the above figure, we can understand the variable 'i' is not used or redefined. We can say 'i' is not live in B2, B3.

The variables, a, b in B2 are live in B3, because these are used in a1, b1.

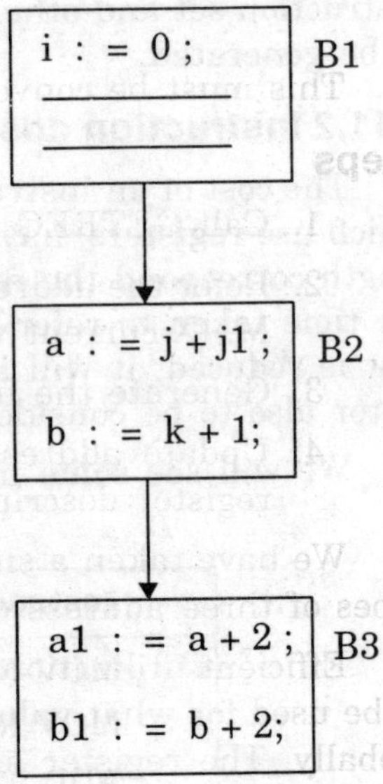

Fig. 4.16 Not live variable

Register descriptor

It is a register that keeps track of the contents of all registers. (Initially all register contents are empty). Whenever necessary the register descriptor will be referenced by symbol table for knowing the details of registers during run time. (Whether a name is live or not live will be available in the register descriptor).

Address descriptor

An address descriptor is a register, which keeps track of addresses of the names, during runtime. This will also be consulted by the symbol table. Addresses of all the names and other registers etc. will be maintained by the address descriptor during the runtime.

Code generation

We will see an example, to know what code generation is actually.

Consider the address code

temp1: = X – Y

The corresponding code generated will be as follows:

```
MOV X RO
SUB Y RO
```

This is the code generated, considering the instruction set of the machine. This code can further be converted into corresponding object code. So we can understand that the term code generation means converting the three address codes into corresponding assembly language code based on the instruction set of the machine. Hence our discussions regarding code generation will be generation of assembly code using the instructions of instruction set of the target machine.

Before we discuss further we will see a function called GETREG, for some convenience.

Getreg

It is a function used in code generation. This function returns an address to keep the value of a variable, say "a". It gives a register to keep the value of any name. More precisely the address of register (say) to the keep the value of the variable.

We see the steps involved for generating code from the three-address codes using the GETREG function.

Consider the three-address code

temp1: = X – Y

This must be converted into corresponding codes (Assembly code).

Steps

1. Call GETREG to store the value of temp1 (address to store the result)
2. Refer the address descriptor if X is available, if not move the value to some location M. (X-current value of X)
3. Generate the instruction OP Y, M (current value of Y)
4. Update address and register descriptors (keep the live information also in the register descriptor).

We have taken a simple type of three-address code for code generation, codes for other types of three address codes can be generated by applying the above steps modified.

Efficient utilization of registers is to be considered for code generation. What registers to be used for what values, is called register allocation. This is to be done locally as well as globally. The register allocation can be done efficiently by using various algorithms, like graph coloring.

Summary

In this chapter all the phases of the compiler are discussed in detail, and also in very simple style. The readers can try to solve some problems using the algorithms given in this chapter. All the major concepts with respect to the design of a compiler have been discussed here in this chapter. The readers can refer the book 'Elements Compiler Design' by the same author for further reference. Please refer the Bibliography, for this book details.

QUESTIONS

Part A

1. Grammar G: E → T + E | T

   T→T*T | F

   F→constant | (E)

   Draw syntax tree for 2 + 3*5.
2. Distinguish between compiler and translator.
3. What is a token?
4. What is a lexical analyzer?
5. What is a parse tree? Give example.
6. Give the associatively of the operator.
7. Give the need for lexical analysis in compilation.
8. Give two types of parsing with example.
9. Define regular expression.
10. Define CFG (or) BNF.
11. Give the valid parse tree representation for id * id + id.

12. What language is generated by the grammar S——> 0S1|01?

13. Give the rules for a regular expression.

14. Give two examples of context free grammar.

15. Give examples for terminals and non terminals.

16. What is the role of lexical analyzer?

17. Define Production rules.

18. What is the unary postfix operator.

19. What do you mean by ambiguity?

20. Define ambiguous grammar.

21. Prove that "if-then-else" grammar is an ambiguous grammar.

22. Construct the syntax tree for a* (b + d)|d.

23. Write a grammar for a simple arithmetic expression.

24. Give the RE for (a) Identifier

(b) Constant

(c) Keyword

25. Define a context free grammar?

26. Write regular definition for the language "All strings of digits with no repeated digit".

27. What is a syntax tree?

28. Difference between parse tree and syntax tree.

29. Define syntax, semantics.

30. Define nondeterministic finite automata.

31. When you say finite automata is deterministic.

32. Draw the transition diagram for identifiers and keywords.

33. Define the term finite automata.

34. Distinguish between NFA and DFA.

35. Give the data structure for representing transition table.

36. Draw NFA for recognizing the language

(ab)* abb.

37. List the tokens in the statement:

(*i*) IF (6.EQU.MAX) GOTO 75

38. How do you justify that LR parsers are attractive?

39. Consider the grammar:

S ———> AS|b

A ———> SA|a

Give the augmented grammar?

40. What is the handle of a right-sentential form.

41. Define operator-precedence grammar.

42. What is operator grammar?
43. Define handle pruning.
44. Define LR grammar.
45. Give the rules for construction of CLOSURE.
46. What do you mean by LALR parsing?
47. Write about the shift-reduce parsing technique with an example.
48. Write Quadruples for the expression?

    –(a+b) * (c+d) – (a+b+c)
49. What information does the symbol table hold?
50. Using syntax directed translation scheme generate the intermediate code for case statement.
51. Define syntactic error.
52. Define semantic rule.
53. Define intermediate text.
54. Differentiate three-address code and quadruples?
55. Explain the syntax-directed translation of case statements.
56. Define symbol tables.
57. What is a self organizing list?
58. What are referencing data?
59. Write about the data structures used to represent the symbol table.
60. Write about call by reference parameter passing mechanism.
61. Define lexical phase error.
62. What is a flow graph?
63. What is address descriptor.
64. What are the applications of DAG?
65. What is DAG?
66. Define code optimization.
67. Define algorithm optimization.
68. Define induction variables.
69. What are the problems in code generation?
70. What is a cross compiler?

Part B

1. Explain the roles performed by lexical analysis and syntax analysis phase of the compiler with examples.
2. Explain the need for code optimization in compilers.
3. Mention the various phases of a compiler and also write their functions briefly.
4. Write a grammar where the sentence are the regular expressions over the alphabet {a,b}

Write a context free grammar that generates all numbers. Numbers can be integer or real, real numbers must be generated either with decimal point or by using E format.

5. Write note on front end and back end of the compilers.

6. The following grammar for if-then-else statements is proposed

stmt ⟶ if expr then stmt | stmt

| if expr then stmt else stmt

Show that the grammar is ambiguous.

7. Write a brief note on context free grammars and regular expression and distinguisl between them.

(*a*) Give example for a context free grammar.

(*b*) What are the properties of regular expression?

(*c*) Test whether the following grammar is ambiguous or not

S ———> S0T | T

T———> Ta F | F

F———> nF | (S) | tf

Where {S.T.F} are non terminals, S the start symbol and 0, a, t, f, n, (,) are terminals.

8. Consider the grammar

S———> (L) | a

L——> L, S | S

What are the terminals, non-terminals and start symbols.

Construct left most and right most derivations and the corresponding parse trees for the following sentence (a, (a, a))

9. Show that the language

(*i*) $L = \{a^n b^n c^n \mid n>=0\}$ is not context free.

(*ii*) A language consists of all strings of 0's and 1's that have odd length,

Write a regular expression for this language.

(*iii*) Write and describe the properties of context free grammar.

(*iv*) Construct a non deterministic finite automaton for the regular expression

(a | b)* abb(a | b)*

(*v*) Show the occurrence of moves made in processing the string ababab

10. Consider the following grammar with set of terminal symbols {a,b}

S→AS

S→b

A—>SA

A —>a

Describe the set of strings generated by the grammar.

11. Explain with the help of a block diagram, the analysis and syntheses phases of a compiler.

12. Draw a NFA accepting the

(*i*) Language for (a|b)*abb

(*ii*) Construct DFA accepting the language.

(*iii*) Explain the minimization of number of states in the DFA.

13. Obtain the DFA for the regular expression. 1*(0|01)* and try to minimize the states.

14. Construct a DFA for the regular expression R = (a|b) * abb (a|b)

15. Design a minimal DFA for the following regular expression (0/1)* 0/1

16. Construct a DFA for the regular expression R = (a/b)*abb(a/b)*

17. Discuss the algorithm for converting a given regular expression into Min.DFA.

(*i*) Distinguish between a deterministic Finite Automaton (DFA) and a deterministic finite automaton [NDFA].

18. Construct a deterministic finite state automaton for the regular expression.

L = (0/1)*011

19. Write an algorithm to construct a deterministic finite automaton from a non-deterministic finite automaton and explain.

20. Specify the lexical form of numeric constants in C language.

21. Write the algorithm for constructing a NFA from a regular expression and generate the NFA for the regular expression

(*i*) 1*(0/01)*

(*ii*) Minimize the DFA represented for the following transition table :

State	input (a)	symbols (b)
(Start) A	B	C
B	B	D
C	B	C
D	B	E
(Accept) E	B	C

22. Write the algorithm for minimizing the number of states of a DFA.

23. Construct a transition diagram to accept the set of tokens shown below.

1. while
2. do
3. end
4. begin
5. else
6. if
7. then
8. begin

24. Describe the LR passing algorithm.

25. What is the drawback of top-down parsing? Explain.

26. Eliminate left-recursion from the following grammar:

(*i*) S———> a | ^ | (T)

(*ii*) T———> T, S | S and

(*iii*) Find out if the transformed grammar is LL (1)

27. Write down the operator precedence passing algorithm.

28. Explain the algorithm of top-down passing with example.

29. Explain the methodology used in constructing a parse tree.

30. Construct the LR (0) items and SLR parser to parse the I/P string

"id*id+id "successfully (Assume the grammar)

31. Distinguish between top-down parsing and bottom-down parsing by means of examples.

32. Explain the algorithm for the construction of predictive parser.

33. Explain the implementation of syntax directed translator with example.

34. Describe about the contents of symbol table.

35. Define three address codes, triples and indirect triples with examples.

36. Describe the methods of translating assignment statements.

37. Describe a syntax directed translation scheme to generate translations for the flow of control constructs.

38. Outline the symbol table organization for a block-structured language.

(*i*) Generate the code for the following three-address code sequence

(*ii*) T: = –B

(*iii*) U: = A – C

(*iv*) V: = T + U

(*v*) W: = V + U

39. What are benefits of having an intermediate code generator?

For the productions:

S ——> id: = E

E —> E+E | id

Give the syntax-directed translation scheme for 3 address codes.

40. Give the translation of three-address code for the following statement:

1. While a < b do

if c < d then

x: = y + z

else

x:=y – z

41. Explain the different kinds of errors handled by the compliers.

42. Explain the methods of parameter passing in a programming Language

43. Explain the syntax directed translation and give the parse tree and translations for the expression (6+29)*3.

44. Discuss the various operations that can be performed on an symbol table.

45. Construct a syntax directed translator that will convert an infix code into post fix code.

46. Convert the following statement

(i) A: = (B+C) * E + (B+C) * F-into triple, indirect triple andquadruple form. Explain how the postfix notation is evaluated using stack.

(ii) Obtain quadruples, triples and indirect triples for the expression:

–(a+b) * (c+d) + (a+b+c).

47. Write a detailed study on code generation

48. Explain how the code optimization done in C.

49. Describe about the loop optimization

50. Write down the algorithm for partitioning a sequence of three-address statements into basic blocks.

51. Explain a simple code generation algorithm.

52. Explain the need for code optimization in compilers.

53. Explain with simple example machine dependent optimizations?

54. What are the roles of basic blocks in code optimization?

55. List the various optimization applied at the code generation phase with simple examples.

56. Explain how common sub-expressions are eliminated in code optimization.

57. What are the factors to be considered in the task of code generation?

58. Describe target code generation phase of a compiler.

59. Describe the organization of a code optimizer.

CHAPTER 5

ASSEMBLERS

Blessed are the merciful,
For they shall obtain mercy.

5.1 INTRODUCTION

This chapter discusses the functions of assembler in detail. We will see the design of an assembler and also the data structures used for the construction of the assembler. This section discusses single pass and two pass assembler design with some example assembly programs written for 8085/8086 architectures. This chapter discusses all the features of assembler based on TASM and MASM assemblers. After reading this chapter the reader will be familiar with the concepts of an assembler and will be able to design an assembler.

5.2 ASSEMBLERS

Assembler is a program, which translates Assembly Language Program (ALP) into machine language program (object program). It places the object program in the secondary memory.

The functions of the assemblers can be understood from the Fig. 5.1. The assembler receives the assembly language program as input and converts into the corresponding object program. It also provides the information to the loader. The loader places this object code into the main memory during execution. There are various loading schemes available. The loaders are discussed in detail in the chapter 7.

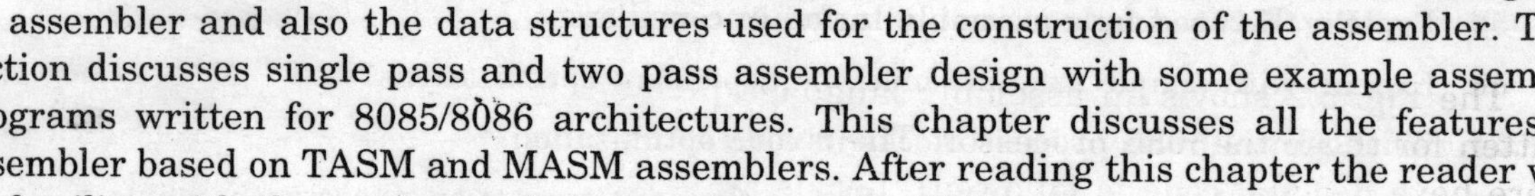

Fig. 5.1 Assembler

Let us try to understand the functions of assemblers in detail, which can help in the design of assembler. The assembler does receive an assembly language program as its input. The output should be an object program (corresponding to the ALP). This will be placed generally in the secondary memory. This will be again loaded placed in the main memory for execution of the program by the loader. So the assembler has to also generate necessary information to the loader. In order to understand how translation is done we consider the following example ALP. This ALP is written based on the instruction set of 8085 processor. (There are various examples for assembly language programs available, which are written for different architectures. This example follows the mnemonics and opcode of 8085 instruction set).

Example 5.1

Address	*Mnemonics*	*Hex machine Code*	*Comments*
8800	SUB A	97	// Clear the accumulator
8801	MVI A, 02	3E 02	// Move 02 to accumulator
8803	MVI B, 03	06 03	// Move 03 to B register
8805	ADD B	80	// Add B with accumulator
8806	STA 8900	32 88 00	// store the result in 8900.
8807	HLT	76	// Halt the execution

Fig. 5.2 A simple assembly language program for adding two numbers

The Fig. 5.2 shows an assembly language program for adding two numbers, which is written for the Intel 8085 processor. The readers can understand how this program works. (Here hexa decimal code is followed). Let us take one instruction from the above program and see how that is converted into its equivalent machine code.

8805 ADD B 80

In this assembly instruction the components present are

- Address 8805
- Mnemonics ADD B and
- Hex machine code 80

The equivalent machine code is **'80 8805'**, which is obtained by just integrating the opcode of the assembly instruction and the corresponding address of it. In a similar way the machine language equivalent for the instruction MVI A, 02 is **'3E 0002'**. In this case the operand 02 (data) is readily available, so it can be directly integrated with the opcode 3E. (This type of addressing mode is called immediate addressing.) The similar method is followed for all the assembly instructions in this example program, for obtaining the complete object program, which is given in the Fig. 5.3.

Address	*Mnemonics*	*Opcode*	*Object code* (Hex decimal form)	(Binary form)
8800	SUB A	97	97	**1001 0111**
8801	MVI A, 02	3E 02	3E0002	**0011 1110**
				0000 0000
				0000 0010

8803	MVI B, 03	06 03	060003	**0000 0110**
				0000 0000
				0000 0011
8805	ADD B	80	808805	**1000 1000**
				0000 0101
8806	STA 8800	32 88 00	328800	**0011 0010**
				1000 1000
				0000 0000
8807	HLT	76	76	**0111 0110**

Fig. 5.3 A simple assembly language program for adding two numbers with the object code.

In the Fig. 5.3 the object program is given in bold face letters. We can understand what the process, from the above example is. We can also understand for translating the assembly code into machine code, two things are important. They are:

1. Operation to be performed (Opcode)
2. Operand or address of the operand.

The equivalent machine code can be obtained for any assembly code by just integrating the operation code (Opcode) and operand or address of the operand. Address is specified directly in the instruction itself or specified using different addressing schemes like immediate addressing, indexed addressing. Sometimes the operands are stored in the labels (like variable names), then those addresses of the labels are considered for translating into the corresponding machine code.

The assembler must place the object code into the secondary memory or any output device. This object program will be loaded into the main memory for execution later by the loader. The assembler must pass the name of the program on to the loader. Before proceeding further, some other concepts are introduced in the subsequent section, which, will help in understanding the design of the assembly process.

5.3 ASSEMBLER DIRECTIVES

These are the instructions present in the source program used to instruct the assembler to perform certain actions during the translation of a program. These are not translated into machine language instructions. The assembler directives are also called 'pseudo instructions'. These are not the instructions for the processors, but for assemblers. The assembler directives discussed are from MASM assembler for the Intel family of architectures. These assembler directives are used in Intel 8086 macro assembler (ASM86), Borland Turbo Assembler (TASM), and IBM macro assembler (MASM).

Example 5.2:

```
ORG 8000H
  _____
  _____
END
```

ORG directive allows to set the location counter to any address. The statement **ORG** 8000H instructs the assembler to set the location counter 8000H. The statement END instructs the end of the program. The statements following this directive will not consider for translation.

ASSUME

The ASSUME directive is used to instruct the assembler the name of the logical segment to be used for a specified.

Example:

ASSUME CS: CODE. This statement tells the assembler, the instructions for a program are in the code segment.

ASSUME DS: DATA. This statement tells the assembler, the data for the instructions of a program are in the data segment.

SEGMENT

The SEGMENT pseudo instruction is used to start a new segment.

ENDS

This is used to terminate the segment usage.

EQU

This is used to give a symbolic name to an expression.

A EQU 2000

In this example the symbol A is assigned the value 2000. The symbol can be used in the expressions and its value is 2000.

DB -Used to allocate storage for words in bytes (8 bits)

DD -Used to declare a variable of type double word or to reserve memory locations, which can be accessed as type double word. (16 bit)

DW -Used to allocate storage for words in 32 bit length

DQ -Used to declare a variable of length 4 words or to reserve memory 4 words of storage in memory. (64 bit)

DT -Used to declare a variable of length 10 bytes or to reserve memory 10 words of storage in memory.

PROC -Used to start a procedure.

ENDP -Used to along with the name of procedure to indicate the end of a procedure to the assembler.

Examples:

Sum ENDP;//End of procedure sum.

DATA ENDS;//End of logical segment CODE.

PUBLIC -Allows a name or symbol to be referenced by other modules.

EXTRN -Used to tell the assembler that names or labels following the directive are in some other assembly module.

INCLUDE	-Allows to include another file in the current program
IF, ELSE, ENDIF	-Used in conditional statements in the usual context.
COMMENT	-Allows the user to change comment delimiter other than semi colon.
PAGE	-Used to generate page breaks.
END	-Used to terminate the assembly program.

There are some more assembler directives, but some of the important directives only discussed above.

5.4 FORWARD REFERENCE

It is a reference of a label (variable name), which is defined later in the program. Consider the following simple program in 8086:

Example 5.3:

```
CODE    SEGMENT
        ASSUME CS: CODE
        JMP XXYY
        NOP
        NOP
XXYY:   MOV AX, 0000H
        NOP
CODE    ENDS
        END
```

This is simple program in written for Intel 8086 processor. This is a delay program. In the above program there is a JMP statement to the statement labeled 'XXYY'. In this case there is reference to a label named 'XXYY', which is defined later in the program. This is called forward reference. This is also called forward jump. This causes some problem in translation of assembly program into object program. There can be backward reference or backward jump possible in the program. This is reference to a label or symbol, which is defined already in the program.

The forward references cause problems during the assembly. During the assembly process, the assembler reads the instructions from the source program and translates them one after another. As it is discussed already, the assembler integrates the opcode and address of each instruction. In the case of an instruction having forward reference, the address will not be readily available. The address is actually defined later, after the particular instruction. See the instruction 'JMP **XXYY**' in the example 5.3. The label is defined later in the program. This causes problem in the assembly process. The assembly cannot be done till the address is known. This is called forward reference problem. This problem is handled by some suitable mechanisms in the assemblers. These discussed in detail in the subsequent sections. The backward references do not cause such problems. In fact they are easy to handle in assemblers.

5.5 TYPES OF ASSEMBLERS

The assemblers can be of any one of the following types:

1. Single pass assemblers
2. Two pass assemblers and
3. Multi pass assemblers.

Pass is a terminology used in system software. *Each reading of a program (source or any program in concern) can be called as a pass.* The assembly process can be done within a pass, if so, such assemblers are single pass assemblers. If the assembly is done two passes, then those assemblers are called two pass assemblers. The translation of the assembly language program can be done in several passes. Such assemblers are called multi pass assemblers. In this book the two pass assemblers are given more importance, since these are widely used.

5.5.1 Single Pass Assemblers

The entire translation of assembly language program into object program is done in only one pass. The source program is read only once. These are also called as 'one pass assemblers'. These assemblers suffer the problem of forward reference. Handling the forward reference in a single pass assembler is difficult. This type of assemblers avoids forward references. But in reality the forward references cannot be completely eliminated.

The object code can be produced in the single pass assemblers in two different ways. In the first way the object code is directly loaded into the main memory for execution. Here no loader is required. This type of loading scheme is 'compile and loading scheme', which is in detail discussed in the chapter 7.

In the second way the object program is stored in the secondary memory. This object program will be loaded into the main memory for execution later as necessity arises. Here a separate loader program is necessary. There are various loading schemes available. These are also discussed in detail in the chapter 7.

The forward reference problem is also handled to some extent in single pass assemblers. The assembler scans the source assembly language program, instruction by instruction and translates them in machine codes. If there is an instruction, which has a forward reference, the assembler leaves the address of that particular symbol (operand) and proceeds further. This symbol is entered in the symbol table and marked as undefined. There is another list of instructions, which uses this symbol, is also maintained. In that list this particular instruction is also included. When the symbol definition is encountered the assembler inserts the address in the symbol table. The symbol table is discussed in detail the next section. The assembler also inserts the address to the instructions, which use this symbol in the list of forward references. This is how the forward reference problem is handled in the single pass assemblers in a single pass. The forward reference problem is conveniently handled in the two pass assemblers. If undefined symbols are encountered after reaching the end of the statement, then the assembler generates the error messages. After translating all the instructions, the object program is used with and without the use of loaders. The control is transferred to the start of the object program for execution.

An assembler, which goes through an assembly language program only once, is known as One-pass assembler. It suffers from forward reference problem. This is faster because they scan the program only once. This does not have many features supported by the two pass assemblers.

5.5.2 Two Pass Assemblers

The two pass assemblers are widely used and the translation process is done in two passes. The two pass assemblers resolve the problem of forward references conveniently. The design of two passes assemblers and other concepts like symbol table management and location counter processing are discussed in the section 5.6. An assembler, which goes through an assembly language program twice, is called a two pass assembler. During the first pass it collects all labels. During the second pass it produces the machine code for each instruction and assigns address to each of them. It assigns addresses to labels by counting their position from the starting address. It provides many features than the single pass assembler. It is widely used.

5.5.3 Multi Pass Assemblers

If the assembly process is done more than two passes then those assemblers are called as *multi pass assemblers*. One reading of a program (source program or any program in concern) can be called as a pass. In assemblers the passes are necessary to solve the problem of forward references. In order to process the entire symbol definitions several passes are made over the source program.

5.6 DESIGN OF TWO PASS ASSEMBLERS

The design of two pass assemblers is discussed hereunder. The design of two pass assemblers involves the design of Pass 1 and Pass 2. The functions of two pass assemblers are also discussed. The functions of pass 1 and pass 2 are given below:

Pass 1 of the Two Pass Assembler

It scans the assembly language program completely and analyses the same. This phase can be also called as **Analysis Phase.** The assembler analyses the assembly language program considering the following factors:

1. Symbols and labels
2. Mnemonics and
3. Declarations.

The assembler uses the location counter, mnemonics table for the pass1. It generates intermediate representation of the source code (IR) and symbol table. The symbol table will maintain the details of symbols.

Functions of Pass 1 of the Two Pass Assembler

1. Tracks the location counter
2. Generates the symbol table by determining the symbols, labels and their addresses
3. Generates the Literal Table (LT)
4. Finds the length of assembly level instructions from mnemonics table
5. Processes the assembler directives
6. Finally generates the intermediate representation of the source program.

Pass 2 of the Two Pass Assembler

This phase only generates the object code of the source program. It uses the intermediate representation from the pass 1 and symbol table. It actually synthesizes the outputs of the pass 1 and opcodes to generate the object code. This pass can also be called as **Synthesis Phase.** It just integrates the opcode and addresses. It uses the symbol table, literal table, mnemonics table and intermediate representation of the ALP from Pass1. The function of Pass2 is to generate the assembly listing. It should also generate some information needed by the loader and linkers for linking up procedures assembled at different times into a single executable file and loading into the main memory.

Functions of Pass 2 of the Two Pass Assembler

1. Finds out the machine codes (Opcodes) for the assembly level instructions from the mnemonics table
2. Finds out the addresses of the symbols from the symbol table and substitutes them in the assembly sequence
3. Processes the assembler directives
4. Generates the object code sequence
5. Generates necessary information to the loader.

These are details pertinent to the functions of the two pass assembler. In the subsequent sections, other design concepts are discussed. The section 5.7 discusses about the data structures used for the design of the two pass assembler. The symbol table management and location counter processing are also addressed in detail in the subsequent sections.

5.7 DATA STRUCTURES FOR TWO PASS ASSEMBLER CONSTRUCTION

This section discusses about the data structures used for the construction of the two pass assembler.

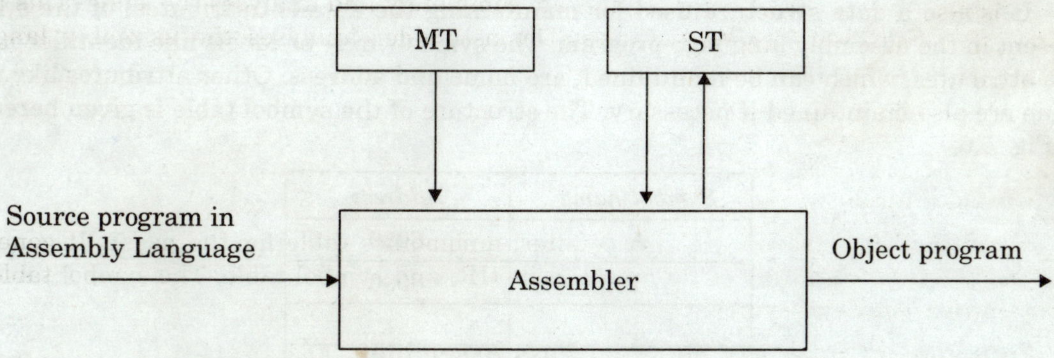

MT - Machine Table

ST - Symbol Table

Fig 5.4 Assembler with machine table and symbol table

It is understood that how the data structures machine table and symbol table are used in the assemblers from the Fig. 5.4. This will also help in understanding the functions of assembler in a better way. The data structures used in the assembler are given below:

1. Mnemonics Table (**MT**)
2. Symbol Table (**ST**)

3. Pseudo Instruction Table (**PIT**)
4. Location Counter (**LC**)
5. Literal Table (**LT**)

We will discuss every data structure and its function in detail in the subsequent sections.

Mnemonics Table (MT)

It is a data structure used for maintaining the details (attributes) about the instructions of instruction set of any machine. It will have mnemonics of the instructions, corresponding hexadecimal opcode and the length of the instruction. The structure of the mnemonics table is given hereunder in the Fig. 5.5.

Mnemonics	*Opcode*	*Length*
SUB B	97	1
ADD B	80	1
...	...	...
HLT	76	1

Fig. 5.5 Mnemonics table organization

The mnemonics table maintains other information too, if necessary, like format of the instruction apart from the above mentioned details. This table can also be called as machine Code Table machine opcode table.

Symbol Table (ST)

It is also a data structure used for maintaining the details (attributes) of the symbols present in the assembly language program. The symbols may be labels like identifier names. The attributes, which can be maintained, are name and address. Other attributes like scope, value are also maintained if necessary. The structure of the symbol table is given hereunder in Fig. 5.6.

Symbol name	*Address*
A	8080
B	8090
...	...
C	8100

Fig. 5.6 Symbol table organization

The data structures, here, refer to the arrangement of data. The data pertinent to mnemonics table and symbol table are to be maintained in this case and also efficiently. There are many data structures available. The suggested data structure for both can be Hash Table, because of the efficiency in insertion and retrieval.

Pseudo Instruction Table (PIT)

Sometimes the assemblers maintain a separate data structure called Pseudo Instruction Table (PIT). This table maintains the details of the Pseudo instructions or assembler directives like ORG, END, ASSUME and others.

Location Counter (LC)

Location Counter is another data structure used to keep the address of the next memory word. LC needs to know the length of different instructions (for incrementing), hence MT (Mnemonics Table) can be included to have the length of the instruction. The process of maintaining the address of the next memory word can be called as 'LC processing'. The location counter is also called as instruction counter. It is a variable, which keeps track of the execution-time address of the instruction being assembled.

Literal Table (LT)

Constants for which the assembler automatically reserves memory are called literals. A literal is an operand that states the required value directly in an instruction. It is alternative to defining a constant elsewhere in the program and then using a label to refer to it. The literals improve the readability of a program by making the value of the constant apparent in the source statement. Pass1 of the assembler builds the 'Literal Table'. This will maintain the details about the literals used in the source program like names and values. Whenever a literal is encountered, new entry will be made in the literal table. At the end of the first pass this literal table sorted in order to remove the duplicates. The machines, which have immediate instructions, will not use literals (E.g. 'MVI' in 8085). In the assembler program the literals must be explicitly specified by using some notations. This is to distinguish between the literal and other symbols and constants.

Literal Name	Address
C	8080
D	8090
...	...
E	8100

Fig. 5.7 Literal table organization

5.8 SYMBOL TABLE MANAGEMENT

The symbol tables are most important data structures in the design of the translators like compilers and assemblers. The symbol table maintains the attributes of the symbols used in the source program. The maintenance of the symbol table is called symbol table management. This is also called as book keeping.

The symbol table keeps track of address, scope, binding information and other attributes of the symbols. The symbol may be a name of an identifier and the like program segments. There will be entries in the symbol table for any name in the source program. The attributes like scope, binding information will vary as the program is being executed. So the symbol table has to be maintained dynamically. There will be new entries of any name during the run-time. If the size of symbol table is to be allotted statically, it should foresee the changes in the symbol table entries and accordingly the size has to be allocated. Sometimes there will be new names also have to be considered.

The symbol table entries are names and their attributes only. In a programming language there will be some keywords or reserved words, and names of the programming segments like variables should not have key words. So the symbol tables should have reserved words like variables should not have key words. So the symbol tables should have reserved words or key words so as to check the names from the source program when encountered.

The source program sometimes have the same name assigned to two different program segments, for example the 'diff' is the name of a (scalar) variable; and the same name may be available variable from array too; 'sco' may be a local variable of function fun1 and it will also another local variable of a function say fun2. So the symbol table must have to separate those things into different entities. There can be a separate entry for each entity.

The names can be stored in the symbol table using fixed sized arrays or dynamically using pointers. The storage location is also to be allotted to names available in the symbol table *i.e.*, memory for a name of a programming segment used in the source program.

The data structures for symbol tables can be:

1. Linear list and
2. Hash tables.

Some of these data structures discussed in the following section.

5.8.1 Linear List

This data structure is used to implement the symbol table is a very simple way. The symbol table keeps the names and their attributes. If any new name is encountered that also to be considered.

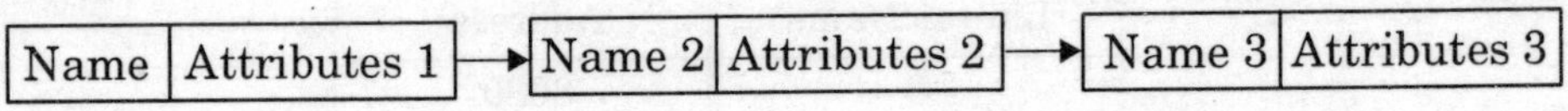

Fig. 5.8 Linear list having the symbol table entrys

Each name and its attributes can collectively be considered as a separate entity. These entities can be made available in a list as shown in Fig. 5.8. The end of the list is left opened to add new symbols (names).

5.8.2 Hash Tables

This data structure can also be used to implement the symbol table. Hashing generally uses good searching techniques. There are many hash functions available. In the symbol table open hashing technique is used, where open refers to open *i.e.*, no limit. It can be used to add more entries. Let us see a simple example for hashing.

Consider the following string 'JOSEPH'. The character J is 10th alphabet in English, and O is 15th alphabet. The numbers of all the characters can be found and can be added together as shown below:

J - 10
O - 15
S - 19
E - 05
P - 16
H - 08
TOTAL → 73

The string can be stored in the location 73 or mapped to the location 73. This is simple hashing technique. In the implementation of symbol table also hashing techniques can be used. In our case the data structure will have:

1. Pointers to symbol table entries
2. Symbol table entries for names

The pointers will point the names in symbol table entries. These are headers to the names. These are obtained by the hash function. These are actually hashed values. The symbol table entries are the names and their attributes. Each name is maintained in a list. This list can be dynamically maintained.

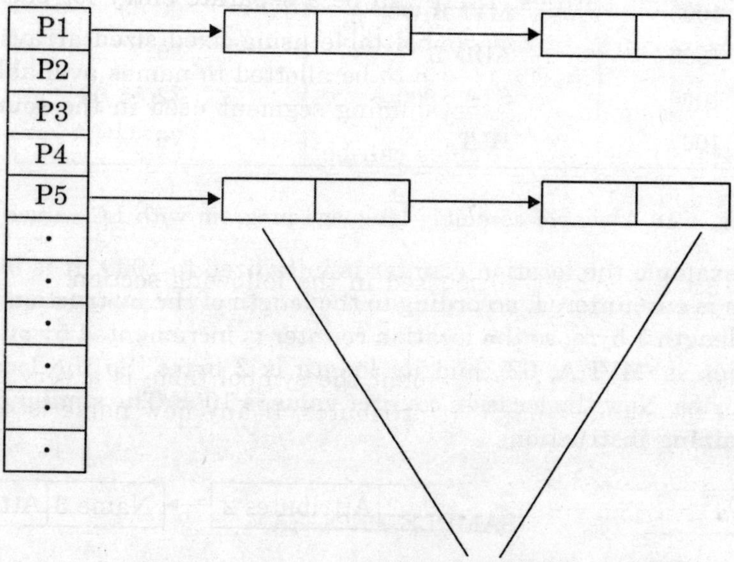

Fig. 5.9 Hash table organization

This type of data structure has better performance over the list in handling the operations like searching, insertions and queries.

In a symbol table there will be lot of entries depending upon the source program. There have to be operations like searching, inserting and other queries, done in the symbol table.

If the entries are less, searching can be easily done. If there are more entries then the searching time will be more. The symbol table operations may not be optimally done for large sized symbol tables.

5.9 LOCATION COUNTER

The location counter is another important data structures used in the assembler design. It keeps track of the address of the next memory word. Its function of tracking the address of the next memory word is called **LC processing.** It is generally initialized to zero. If the memory is already occupied up to 1000 KB means then the location counter will be initialized to 1000. Then during the assembly of every instruction, the location counter is incremented according to the length of the instruction.

Location counter is really helpful in handling the jump and branch instructions. The LC processing can be explained with the help of an example. Consider the example given below. The location counter is initialized 1000.

Example 5.4:

Location Counter	Mnemonics	Opcode (Hex decimal Form)
1000	SUB A	97
1001	MVI A, 02	3E 02
1003	MVI B, 03	06 03
1005	ADD B	80
1006	STA 8900	32 88 00
1007	HLT	76

Fig. 5.10 A simple assembly language program with LC values

In the above example the location counter is initialized to 1000. It is incremented each time an instruction is encountered, according to the length of the instruction. The instruction 'SUB A' is having length 1 byte, so the location counter is incremented by one byte *i.e.,* 1001. The next instruction is 'MVI A, 02', and its length is 2 bytes. So the location counter is incremented by 2 bytes. Now the location counter value is 1003. The similar process repeated for the other remaining instructions.

Example 5.5:

SAMPLE PROGRAM

```
          ORG       4000H
TOTAL:    MOV       AX, 2000H;     load address of data area
          MOV       DS, AX;        Init data segment register
          MOV       AL, 0;         clear result
          MOVBL,    16;            init loop counter
          MOV       SL, 0;         init data pointer
ADDUP:    ADD       AL, [SI];      add data value to result
          INC       SI;            increment data pointer
          DEC       BL;            decrement loop counter
          JNZ       ADDUP;         jump if counter not zero
          MOV       [SI], AL;      save sum
          RET;                     and return
          END
```

The assembler output with location counter values

```
1     4000                              ORG    4000H
2     4000    BB    OO20     TOTAL;     MOV    AX, 2000H
3     4003    8E    D8                  MOV    DS, AX
4.    4005    B0    00                  MOV    AL, 0
5.    4007    B3    10                  MOV    BL, 16
6.    4009    BE    0000                MOV    SI, 0
```

7.	400C	02	04	ADDUP;	ADD	AL, [SI]
8.	400E	46			INC	SL
9.	400F	FE	CB		DEC	BL
10.	4011	75	F9		JNZ	ADDUP
11.	4013	88	04		RET	
12	4015	CB			END	

In the above example, a sample 8086 program is taken and it is converted into the corresponding object program (Hexa decimal form) by the assembler. The location counter is initialized to the address 4000. The output will be generated by the assembler.

5.10 FORWARD REFERENCE PROBLEM IN TWO PASS ASSEMBLERS

In this section the forward reference problem in two pass assemblers are discussed. How this is solved is addressed in this section. This can be handled in two ways. It is obvious that the two pass assembler makes two passes (reading twice) over the source program.

In the first way, during the first pass the definitions of symbols, labels are identified and stored in a table called symbol table. The symbol table keeps the addresses of the symbols, which are having forward reference problems. The addresses are readily available for inserting into the assembly instructions. In the second pass the instructions can be assembled. This is simple method of solving the forward reference problem, but requires another pass (second) over the source program.

In the second way, it generates the intermediate representation of the source program in the first pass. This intermediate representation is stored in the memory. This representation has the addresses of the symbols having forward references. The second pass is made over the intermediate representation not on the source program. It reduces extra I/O operation unlike in the previous approach. But this method occupies extra memory.

A simple project is developed in C++ language for the implementation of the two pass assembler is given in the appendix A. This is developed for the 8085 microprocessor. The reader can refer the same for some more insight into the subject.

5.11 ALGORITHM FOR THE TWO PASS ASSEMBLER

In this section algorithms for the pass1 and pass2 of the two pass algorithm are given. The algorithms are based on the concepts discussed above.

Algorithm for Pass 1 of the Two Pass Assembler

Input

Assembly language program (Source program), Mnemonics Table (MT) Pseudo Instruction Table (PIT).

Output: Symbol Table, Literal Table

1. Read the source program
2. Check for labels and symbols:

   2.1 If present store them in the symbol table along with the contents of the location counter. Then read the next instruction.

3. If not check for assembler directives (Pseudo opcodes):
   3.1 If present and are DB, DW, DD then determine the memory size needed, accordingly update the LC. Then read the next instruction.
   3.2 If the assembler directive is EQU then determine the memory size and initialize, accordingly update the LC. Then read the next instruction.
   3.3 If the assembler directive is ENDS then check for the assembler directive END.

   If so go to Pass2, else go for initializing the LC for the next segment. Then read the next instruction.

   If not read the next instruction.
4. If not then search the Mnemonics Table (MT) for the opcode for the corresponding assembly level instruction.
5. Get the length of that instruction.
6. If literals present then store the literals and their values in the Literal Table (LT) for pass2.
7. Update the location counter, then read the next instruction.

Algorithm for Pass 2 of the Two Pass Assembler

Input

Copy of the assembly language program (Source program), Mnemonics Table (MT), *Pseudo Instruction table (PIT), symbol table, literal table,*

Output: Object Code and Information to the Loader.

1. Read the source program
2. Check for assembler directives (Pseudo opcodes):
   2.1 If the assembler directive is EQU then allot the memory address and initialize, then determine the size.
   2.2 If the assembler directives are DB, DW then allot the memory addresses, else if DUP then initialize, if not determine size.
   2.3 If the assembler directive is END prepare and store load information, then store the object module and exit.
   2.4 If the assembler directive is not END read the next instruction.
3. If it is assembly level instruction search the Mnemonics Table (MT) and get the Instruction length, type and opcode.
4. Determine the operand codes
5. Decide the code of complete instruction
6. Update the location counter, read the next instruction.

This algorithm is based on the Intel instruction set. This algorithm is simple to understand. This is self-explanatory. The algorithm gives a broader sketch of the assembly process. The implementation details will vary depending on the architecture, instruction set and the assembler tool used.

5.12 ADDITIONAL FEATURES OF ASSEMBLERS

In this section some more additional features of the assemblers are discussed. These are also very important for the design and construction of assemblers. The addressing modes and the instruction formats also play an important role in the conversion of source program into object program. In the assembly process, the opcode and operand is to be combined (in a raw sense). If the operand is not explicitly specified then the address is to be combined with the opcode. The address is specified using some memory reference instructions sometimes. Here we can understand one thing clearly *i.e.*, address computation is one important thing for the assembly process. These concepts discussed in this section.

Immediate Addressing

The Intel architectures support immediate addressing. Consider the following example:

MVI A, 02

This instruction has the data in the instruction itself. The letter "I" in "MVI" stands for immediate. We know that combining the opcode and operand is assembly in a raw sense. So here it can be easily done. The opcode for "MVI" will be readily available in the Machine opcode Table (MT). The operand is '02'. So the corresponding assembler output will be as follows:

3E 02

In order to distinguish the immediate addressing from other instructions in Intel architectures, all the immediate addressing instructions will have the letter "I" as in "MVI".

Direct Addressing

In this addressing, the conversion is very simple the address of the operand is readily available. So this can be easily combined for getting the equivalent object code.

For Example:

MOV C, A

In this case the corresponding assembler output will be as follows.

4F

Memory Reference Instructions

In this case some memory reference instructions are used. So the address calculation is not very simple. Such instructions use base registers or index registers. The displacement or offset is to be added with the base or index value, to compute the effective address. Here the base register or index register value and offset or displacement values should be known and made available for the assembler to do the assembly. The base register values can be maintained in a table called "Base Table" (BT). This phenomenon can be followed for all such types of instructions. The base table will maintain the details of the instructions using base registers and index registers.

Relocation

Relocation is another important concept to be considered for the assembly process. The need for relocation and other concepts are discussed in the operating systems and loaders chapters in detail.

There are blocks of program units available in a program. These are called as program blocks. The program blocks are individual pieces of the object code that are independent of one another and handled separately by the loader. The best example is a segment in the Intel architectures.

In Intel 80×86 architectures segments are available. The output of the assembly process will be a different object module for the corresponding segment of the code. The segments can be initialized by using loctation counters. There can be many location counters used in a program. In the modern operating systems using multiprogramming and multitasking concepts, Swapping the memory blocks in and out of main memory is possible. So the program blocks have to be located and relocated. So the address occupied in the main memory by a block will keep varying. This is done by the operating system along with the loader. So the runtime address of the program unit will be decided by the loader only and also at the runtime. There are some protection mechanisms available, which are already discussed in the operating system chapter. This can be done by changing the value of the location counter for the particular segment. This is done by the loader at the runtime. The Pass2 of the assembler solves the symbolic references and prepares the *Map* for a particular assembly language program. This map will have the information as whether the segment is relocatable or not? And also other details like size of the segment, relocatable labels, relocatable data are also prepared by the Pass2 of the assembler. These are maintained by symbol table like data structures.

5.12.1 External Symbols and External Symbol Table

There can be external symbols also. In a program there are several functions or subroutines. In a very broader sense a program can be defined as a set of procedures or functions. The subroutines are independent program units or blocks. These are sometimes called as control sections. There can be symbols present in different control sections. The symbols in one subroutine are said to be external to another subroutine. The reference of one symbol from another subroutine is called as external reference.

The details of external symbols can be maintained in a data structure called external symbol table. All the concepts to symbol table are same the external symbol tables also. The only difference is they are external.

The assembler directives used for this purpose are given below:

PUBLIC - Allows a name or symbol to be referenced by other modules.

EXTRN - Used to tell the assembler that names or labels following the directive are in some other assembly module.

The assembler directive 'PUBLIC' defines a symbol, which can be used publicly and any module can use the symbols as external symbols.

The assembler directive 'EXTRN' is used to specify some external symbols are used in this module. The external symbols (defined outside of the module) are specified by the keyword 'EXTRN' followed by the external symbols.

Summary

In this chapter the basic concepts of an assembler are introduced first. The concepts are based on MASM and TASM assemblers. Then various types of assemblers are addressed in this chapter. The design of a two pass assembler with examples is discussed in a very simple style. The problem of forward reference problem and the solutions are also discussed. There are few example programs, which are based on the instruction set of Intel 8085 and 8086 processors. The algorithm for the two pass assembler is given in a simplified manner, which will be of great help to the readers, to understand the two pass assembler design. Some more additional features with respect to the assemblers are also discussed at the end of the chapter.

QUESTIONS

Part A

1. What is an assembler?
2. What are the functions of an assembler?
3. What is an assembler directive?
4. Give examples for assembler directives.
5. What are pseudo opcode?
6. What is a pass in assemblers?
7. What is forward reference problem in assembler?
8. What are the functions of passes in two pass assembler?
9. What is the use of symbol table in assembler?
10. What is the structure of literal table in assemblers?
11. What is Location Counter processing?
12. What are the data structures used in two pass assembler design?
13. What are the functions of PASS1 in two pass assembler?
14. What are the functions of PASS2 in two pass assembler?
15. Write note on EQU assembler directive.
16. What is known as literal?
17. Give one simple example for MASM program?
18. What are the tables created and used by the assembler.
19. Why do we need searching and sorting routines in an assembler?
20. List the advantages and disadvantages of a single pass assembler.
21. What is a multi pass assembler?
22. What is hashing?
23. What is an external symbol?
24. What is an external reference?
25. What is a literal table?
26. What is the need for relocation?

Part B

1. Explain the design of two pass assembler in detail with the help of necessary algorithms.
2. Write note on:

   (*a*) Symbol table for assemblers

   (*b*) LC Processing

3. Distinguish between single pass and a two pass assembler. In your opinion, which is preferred? Give reasons.
4. Explain about the data structures used in the design of a two pass assembler and comment on them.
5. What is forward reference problem? Give the solutions for solving the same.
6. What are analysis and synthesis phases of the assembler and explain the same.
7. Give the algorithms for the Pass1 and Pass2 of the two pass assembler and explain.
8. What the features of:
   (*a*) Single pass assembler
   (*b*) Two pass assembler
   (*c*) Multi pass assembler
9. Write note on:
   (*a*) MASM assembler
   (*b*) TASM assembler

CHAPTER 6

MACROS AND MACRO PROCESSORS

Blessed are the peace makers,
For they shall be called sons of god.

6.1 INTRODUCTION

This chapter discusses about macros and macro processors in detail. Before discussing about macros and macro processors, some introduction about preprocessors and subroutines are given, which will help in understanding the concepts of macros and macro processors. The chapter focuses on the design aspects of the macro processor. Moreover the advanced features of the macro processors are also addressed in this chapter.

6.2 PREPROCESSORS AND SUBROUTINES

This section discusses about preprocessors and subroutines. The understanding of these will help to understand the concepts of macros. Some examples are also given for the preprocessors. The discussion on preprocessors is a prerequisite.

Preprocessors

It is a program that processes the source program before it is passed to the compiler. It does preprocessing functions on the source program to make it suitable for compilation. It provides convenience for the programmers. The preprocessor offers several features called preprocessor directives. Some of the preprocessor directives used in C language are:

1. #include directive
2. #define directive and
3. #undef directive

The readers can refer any book on C language for more details on these directives. It is important to note that a macro is preprocessor.

Subroutines

The subroutines are independent program units. These are used in modular programming. Subroutines work independently from the main program. These are compiled separately and linked together and loaded into memory for execution. Subroutines are also called procedures and even functions. Generally these are referred as program modules. Some textbooks refer as control sections. There are some ways transferring the control to the subroutines. Based on the way in which the control is transferred the subroutines can be classified into two types. They are:

1. Open subroutines
2. Closed subroutines.

6.2.1 Closed Subroutines

There is one type of subroutine called closed subroutine, in which the control will be transferred to the subroutine. The subroutine's code will be available outside of the main program. Whenever the program is called, the flow of control will be transferred to that code. Here the control gets affected. The Fig. 6.1 shows how the control is transferred to the subprogram after call statement and also how the control is returned after the execution of the subprogram. In this example, a subroutine "closed ()" is called in the main program. Then the control is transferred to the subroutine "closed ()". The subroutine "closed ()" is executed. Then the control is returned to the main program. This is what happens in case of closed subroutines. Procedures are generally closed subroutines.

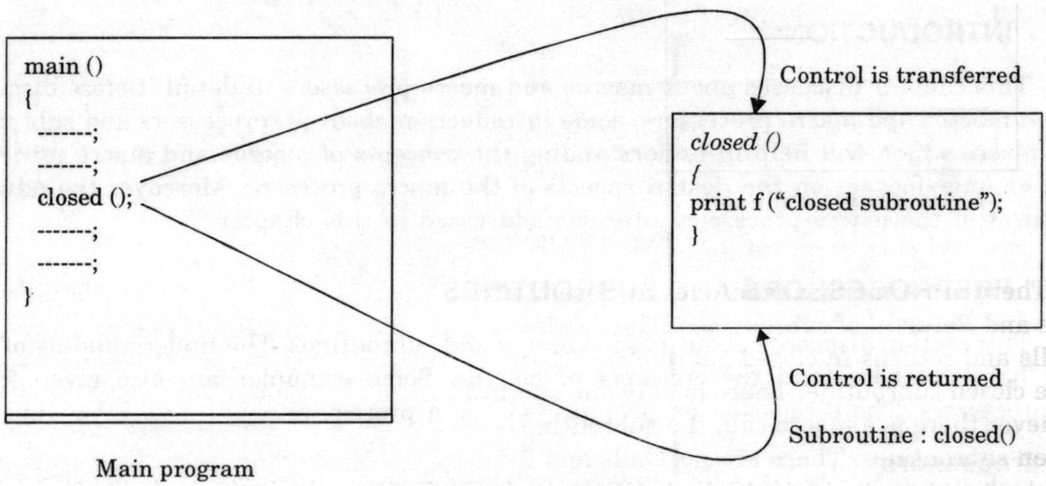

Fig. 6.1 Closed subroutine

6.2.2 Open Subroutines

In this case, the subroutines are executed in a different way. The control does not get affected in any way. Whenever a subroutine is called the subroutine's code is inserted into the main program or in the calling program. The control is not transferred to the subroutine. Such subroutines are called open subroutines. The Fig. 6.2 shows the function of open subroutines. The subroutine "opens ()" in the main program is called, which is actually defined outside. After this call the code for the subroutine "opens ()" is brought to the main program and inserted. This can be understood from the Fig. 6.2. The subroutine is executed, as if it is executed in the original program. The control is not transferred. The flow of control does not get affected in these types of subroutines.

The important thing to note here is "macros are open subroutines". The other concepts are discussed in detail in the subsequent sections.

```
main ()
{
-------;
-------;
opens ();
-------;
-------;
}
```

a. Main program

```
opens ()
{
printf("open subroutine");
}
```

b. Subroutine: opens()

```
main ()
{
-------;
-------;
{
printf("open subroutine");
}
-------;
-------;
}
```

c. After subroutine call

Fig. 6.2 Open subroutine

There are some disadvantages in closed subroutines. A stack is needed to maintain the 'Calls and Returns' of subroutines. The overhead is another disadvantage due to the number of calls and returns in closed subroutine. There must be always a return statement present in the closed subroutine. There is only one subroutine body available. But in case of macros, whenever there is a macro call, the subroutine body will appear. The overhead is less in case of open subroutines. There are no 'Calls and Returns' in open subroutines. There is no need of a stack to keep track of 'Call and Return' statements.

6.3 MACROS

It is discussed already in the previous section, open subroutines are macros. There are some definitions for macros. These are given hereunder:

1. Macro is a name or abbreviation for a part of program (can be a subroutine).
2. A set of codes for a particular operation can be defined as a macro. Defining any subroutine like this is called **macro definition.** This is actually text replacing capability.
3. Macro is an abbreviation for a sequence of operations.
4. A macro represents a commonly used group of statements in the source program.

Macroinstructions are usually considered as an extension of the basic assembler language (assembly language). The macro can be anywhere used in the program. Its occurrence can be called as **macro call.** Macro call is also called macro invocation. There are some differences between the macro call and procedure call. Macro calls are made during the assembly process. The procedure calls are made during the program execution. Whenever there is a macro call the body is inserted into the object program. But for the procedure call only control is transferred. There is no need for any return instruction in case of macros. But there must be a return statement used at the end of every execution of the procedure. The body of the macro appears in the object program for every macro call. The body of the procedure appear only once in the object program.

Example 6.1:

```
EX1     MACRO
        MOV BX, 25
        MUL BX
        ENDM
```

The example 6.1 gives a simple example for a macro. In this macro the 'number 25' is moved to the 'BX' register. This is multiplied with the contents of the accumulator. This particular operation can be frequently executed since it is defined as macro.

6.4 MACRO PROCESSORS

The macro processor is a preprocessor, which handles the macros. Whenever there is macro call the macro processor substitutes the definition in the place of macro call. This is macro expansion. (Whenever there is a macro call, the macro processor replaces it by the macro body and it is called as **macro expansion.**) A macro processor can be considered as an extension of the basic assembler algorithm. Assemblers must pass the name of the macros on to the loader for loading into the main memory for execution. The design of macro processor is not directly related to the architecture of the computer on which it is to run. Macro processors can also be used with high level programming languages, operating system command languages. There are general-purpose macro processors, which are independent of the programming languages.

We will see some examples for macros to understand the concepts clearly. The examples here considered are for C programming language for some easy understanding. Then we will see how the macros are written in assembly languages for Intel architectures. Macroinstruction languages differ significantly from assembly languages and compiled algebraic languages.

6.5 MACROS IN HIGH LEVEL LANGUAGE PROGRAMMING

This section will introduce the macros in the High Level Languages (HLL). This will give some ideas about the macros and their functions. For some convenience the programming language C is taken for the discussion.

```
#define PI 3.14
```

This is a macro definition. The macro processor replaces every occurrence of 'PI' in the program with 3.14. This macro definition can be used in a C program as given below:

Example 6.2

```
#define PI 3.14
main ()
    {
    float r = 2.0;
    area    = PI * r * r;
    printf ("area = %f", area);
    }
```

In the statement **area = PI *r*r,** the macro 'PI' is called. This is a macro call. The macro is expanded or replaced in its occurrence by the macro processor. This is called macro expansion. The macro expanded program will be as given below:

```
#define PI 3.14
main ()
    {
    float r = 2.0;
    area = 3.14 * r * r;
    printf ("area = %f", area);
    }
```

The macros can have arguments. We will see an example for this too. The example

Example 6.3

```
#define AREA(x) (3. 14 * x * x)
main ()
    {
    float r, a;
    scanf ("%f%f",&a,&r);
    a = AREA(r);
    printf ("area = %f", a);
    }
```

In the example 6.3 the macro definition **AREA(x), 'x'** is the argument and in the macro call AREA(r), r is the argument is to be substituted for x , during the macro expansion by the macro processor. The argument 'x' is formal argument (parameter) and the argument 'r' is actual argument. The macro expanded program is given below:

```
#define AREA(x) (3. 14 * x * x)
main ()
    {
    float r, a;
    scanf ("%f%f",&a,&r);
    a = 3.14 * r * r;
    printf ("area = %f", a);
    }
```

6.6 MACROS IN ASSEMBLY LANGUAGE PROGRAMMING

This section discusses about the macros, which are written using the syntax of MASM and TSAM assemblers. These can be run on the Intel architectures. The general syntax for a macro definition is given below:

```
MACRO_NAME MACRO
           ________
           ________
           ________
           ENDM
```

The statement 'MACRO_NAME' is start of the macro and it gives the macro name. The word 'MACRO' indicates that it is a macro. Word 'ENDM' tells the end of the macro. MACRO, ENDM are macro directives, which do the functions similar to the assembler directives. In fact these are assembler directives only. These will not be executed. These give useful information to the macro processor.

Example 6.4

```
ADD1 MACRO
     ADD AX, 25
     ENDM
```

This is a simple macro, which adds the data 25H with the contents of 'AX' register. Whenever this macro is called, this code except the macro directives and the macro name, (MACRO, ENDM, and ADD1) are inserted in the calling place. The above can be called as 'macro definition'. The insertion of this code in the calling place is called 'macro expansion'. The calling of the macro is called 'macro call'.

Example 6.5

```
DISPLAY MACRO
        MOV AH, 9
        INT 21H
        ENDM
```

This is another simple macro is used to display the string, whenever it is called. The statement 'MOV AH, 9' is string display function. The statement 'INT 21H' is for DOS call so that the string is displayed in the CRT.

Example 6.6

```
INTERCHANG MACRO
           MOV EBX, R
           MOV ECX, S
           MOV S, EBX
           MOV R, ECX
           ENDM
```

This simple macro is to interchange the contents of registers EBX, ECX with the variables R and S. The registers are in Intel 80386 architecture.

6.6.1 Macros with Parameters

The macros can have parameters as in subroutines. This expands the scope of the macro for various other situations. The parameters can be formal parameters and actual parameters as in procedures. The formal parameters are present in the macro definition. The actual parameters are the parameters present in the macro calls. The general syntax for such type of macros is given below:

```
MACRO_NAME MACRO formal parameters
           ________
           ________
           ________
           ENDM
```

The keywords 'MACRO' and 'ENDM' are the macro directives. 'MACRO_NAME' is the name of the macro. 'Formal parameters' are listed as it is given in the general syntax. They should be in coincidence with the actual parameters in type and order. The actual parameters will be specified in the macro call. We will see some examples for the macros with parameters.

Example 6.7

```
ADDP MACRO value
     ADD AX, value
     ENDM
```

In this macro, the symbol 'value' is the formal parameter. Let us see a macro call for the above example.

ADDP D

This is a macro call. Here the 'D' is the actual parameter. In this case the actual parameter is replaced with the formal parameters during macro expansion. *Generally the macro definitions will provide the formal parameters and the macro calls will supply the actual parameters.* Whenever a macro is expanded, each formal parameter appearing in the macro body is replaced with the corresponding actual parameter. The actual parameters are placed in the operand field of the macro call.

Example 6.8

```
INTERCHANGP MACRO F1, F2
            MOV EBX, F1
            MOV ECX, F2
            MOV F2, EBX
            MOV F1, ECX
            ENDM
```

Let us see a macro call for this example.

INTERCHANGP R, S

The symbols F1, F2 are formal parameters. The formal parameters F1, F2 will be replaced with the actual parameter R and S respectively during the macro expansion.

There is one more example, which receives the data and adds it to the value of 'AX' register. The data are sent through the formal parameters.

Example 6.9

```
ADD2 MACRO Y
     ADD AX, Y
     ENDM
```

The macro call statement will be given below:

ADD 25.

Due to this macro call, the value 25 will be added with the contents of the contents of the 'AX' register.

6.7 MACRO PROCESSOR DESIGN

In this section the design concepts of macro processors are discussed. Here all the concepts are presented based on MASM and TASM assemblers. The source program is read and is then transformed into another program from which all macro definitions have been removed; and also all the macro calls have also been replaced with the corresponding macro bodies. The output of the macro processor will be an assembly language program containing no macros. Like in assemblers the macro processor can also be designed in two passes. (Each reading of a source program is called a pass). In the first pass all the macro definitions are saved and expanded. The macro body *i.e.,* text is processed in the second pass. The macro processor (some times part of the assembler) treats it, as though it is the original program.

The macro processor is system software. It is actually a program, which is a part of the assembler program. The macro processor is designed in passes. In the design of a macro processor there are two important functions to be considered. They are given below:

1. Saving the macro definitions
2. Expanding the macro calls.

These functions are done in two passes. Here pass refers to reading the source program once. The functions of each pass are given below:

Functions of Pass 1

1. Reads the source program
2. If there is a macro call, stores the definition of the macro in Macro Definition Table (MNT)
3. Stores the macro name in the Macro Name Table (MNT)
4. Prepares the List of formal Arguments (AL) in the macro.
5. Repeats the similar processes for all the other macros.

Functions of Pass 2

1. Reads the source program
2. If there is a macro call, expands the macro with the help of Macro Name Table.
3. Replaces the formal parameters in the Argument List with the actual parameters.
4. Repeats the similar processes for all the other macros.

These are the functions done by the macro processor in two different passes. The next section discusses about the data structures used in the two passes.

6.7.1 Data Structures used Macro Processor Design

There are some important data structures used in the design of a macro processor. These are discussed in detail here under.

Macro Name Table (MNT)

It is a data structure, which maintains the names and the addresses (pointers) where the macro definition is available. This address is helpful to retrieve the macro definition during the macro call.

Argument List (AL)

It also maintains the details about the formal parameters. A list of formal parameters is also maintained. The formal parameters are indicated by some special symbols.

```
MOV EBX, &R
MOV EAX, &S
```

Here 'R', 'S' are formal parameters, and a special symbol '&' is used to precede these parameters so as to indicate that these are formal parameters.

Macro Definition Table (MDT)

It is also a data structure which keeps the macro body *i.e.*, text. The macro body can be retrieved and used during the macro expansion by the macro processor. Whenever a macro definition is encountered, the body is read and stored in the macro definition table.

The functions can be rewritten using the above mentioned data structures as given below:

Functions of Pass 1 of the Macro Processor

- Create the Macro Name Table (MNT), Macro Definition Table (MDT) during Pass1.
- Create a list of formal parameters (AL) in Macro Name Table.

Functions of Pass 2 of the Macro Processor

- During any macro call, reads the macro body from Macro Definition Table (MDT) with the help of Macro Name Table (MNT)
- Extracts the formal parameters from the macro body and replace them by the actual parameters provided in the macro call.

6.8 ADVANCED FEATURES IN MACRO PROCESSORS

Most of the macro processors are having advanced features to make the assembly language program writing convenient. Some of them are discussed in this section.

6.8.1 Conditional Macros

Macros can be expanded based on some conditions. It allows choice in the assembly process. Like in any programming language 'IF....ELSE' structures can be used. Conditional branching can be possible using 'IF' statements. The type of conditions used is listed below:

1. EQ Equal
2. NE Not Equal
3. LT Less Than
4. GT Greater Than
5. LE Less than or Equal
6. GE Greater than or Equal

The following example will show how the IF structures are used in macros.

Example 6.10

```
CMAC1 MACRO
   IF WORDLENTH GT 16
MAC2 MACRO
      ________
      ________
      ENDM
      ELSE
MAC3 MACRO
      ________
      ________
      ENDM
ENDIF
ENDM
```

The usage of IF statements can be understood from the above example. The expansion of the macros MAC2 and MAC3 is dependent on the value of word length of the machine. There is another example for conditional macro, which handles parameters too.

Example 6.11

```
ADDMUL MACRO X
       IF X GT 10
          ADD AX, X
       ELSE
          MUL X
       ENDIF
       ENDM
```

This macro receives the value of 'X' as input. 'X' is either added or multiplied depending on its value.

There are some advantages in conditional macro expansion. It increases the efficiency in execution. It also reduces the memory utilization.

MASM and other assemblers allow nested macros. *If a macro is defined within another macro then it is called nested macro.* This feature is very much useful in assembly language programs.

Example 6.12

```
MACNES MACRO X
       __________
       __________
    IF X GT 100
 MACN1 MACRO
       __________
       __________
       ENDM
       ELSE
 MACN2 MACRO
       __________
       __________
       ENDM
 ENDIF
 ENDM
```

The above example gives an idea about, how the nested macros will be? The macro MACN1 and MACN2 are nested macros. One macro is embedded within another macro.

The macros can be called by other macros. This is similar to calling the procedures in high level languages. As in high level languages the macros can be recursive. If any macro calls itself then such macros are called recursive macros. As in recursive procedures there must be terminating conditions exist in the recursive macros too, in order to stop the indefinite macro running.

6.8.2 Macro Operators

Operators are used in the macros, which help in defining the macro definition. Some of the macro operators used in MASM assemblers are given below:

% Expression

<....> Literal character string

;; Macro comment

& Substitute

The expression operator '%' is used to extract the value of a parameter from the expression, which can further be used in the macro expansion. Consider the following macro.

Example 6.13

```
ADD MACRO Y
    ADD AX, Y
    ENDM
```

Suppose there is a macro call as given below:

ADD % 2 *15

In this case the value passed to the parameter is '2 * 15' = 30. The operator % is to interpret the following expression and the value 30 is to be passed to the parameter 'Y'.

The operator '<....>' is to place a particular character string in macro. For example, consider a string "I am the truth". This can be specified by using the operator '<....>' as follows:

<I am the truth>

This operator is used in conjunction with the substitution operator **'&'.** The substitution operator **'&'** is used to substitute data.

Consider the instruction **"STR&NUM"** and is used in the macro. During the macro expansion the value of NUM is substituted in the instruction. Suppose the value of NUM is 1, and then the instruction will be **STR1.** Similarly every call of the macro, the values of NUM will be substituted.

Example 6.14

```
SUBS MACRO D, R
        SH&D R, 1
        ENDM
```

In the above example the value of 'D' will be substituted in the place of '&' operator. Suppose the macro call is as follows:

SUBS L, AX

Then the resultant macro expansion will be

SHL AX, 1

Note : D = L; R = AX;

The macro comment operator '; ;' is used to indicate comments in the macro definition. As in the programming languages, the comments are used here also; the comments serve a similar purpose. The following macroinstruction gives an idea about how comments are given in macros using this operator.

MOV AL, DATA ;; Load Number.

The **';;'** operator prevents the comments being expanded during macro expansion.

6.8.3 Labels in Macros

The labels are permitted in macros and also used as in the other programming tools. The labels are handled in a different way in MASM assemblers. Whenever there is a label first encountered, this will be treated as a label and its attributes are maintained. This is done during the macro expansion. During the second call, if the same label will be encountered, the assembler will try to treat the same as a new label, which will lead to confusions. This problem must be solved. Declaring the label as local variable solves this problem.

Example 6.15

```
LAB MACRO
    CMP AL, 10
    JNC YYY
    ADD AL, 5
```

```
YYY: ADD AL 30
     ________
     ________
     ENDM
```

The label "YYY" will cause assembly error during the macro expansion in the second macro call. Declaring the label "YYY", as local variable, can solve this problem. The new macro definition will be as given below:

```
LAB  MACRO
     LOCAL YYY
     CMP AL, 10
     JNC YYY
     ADD AL, 5
YYY: ADD AL 30
     ________
     ________
     ENDM
```

Summary

This chapter introduced the basic concepts of macros and macro processors in detail. The macros used in a high level language C are discussed to introduce about low level macros. The macros discussed as examples are written based on the Intel architectures not based on any pseudo code. The design of the macro processor and the data structures used in the design of a macro processor are also discussed in simple style. The macro processor works as part of an assembler. The concepts discussed are based on MASM and TASM (Turbo Assembler), which are designed for Intel architectures. Advanced features of macros are also discussed with examples.

QUESTIONS

Part A

1. Define a macro.
2. What are preprocessors? Give examples.
3. Give examples for macros.
4. What are the differences between macros and subroutines?
5. What are open and closed subroutines?
6. What is macro processor?
7. What are the functions of a macro processor.
8. What are the data structures used in a macro processor.
9. What is macro directive? Give few examples.
10. What are nested macros?

11. Give examples for nested macros.
12. What is general purpose macro processor?
13. Distinguish between macro call and function call.
14. Give one simple example for MASM program.

Part B

1. Explain the functions of macro processor with the help of the algorithms.
2. What the data structures used in the design of macro processor and comment the role of each data structure?
3. Explain the functions of a two pass macro processor in detail.
4. Explain about the conditional macro expansion and recursive macro expansion with suitable examples
5. What are the advanced macro facilities and explain them.
6. Write note on the following:

   (*i*) Microsoft assembler

   (*ii*) Turbo Assembler

CHAPTER 7

LOADERS AND LINKERS

Blessed are the pure in heart,
For they shall see God.

7.1 INTRODUCTION

This chapter discusses about the loaders and linkers. The functions and design of loaders are discussed clearly in this chapter. The types of loaders are also addressed in this section. At the end of this chapter the reader will be able to understand the concepts about the loaders and linkers and also the concepts involved in the design of loaders and linkers.

Loader is a program (can be a sub program) that loads the object program from the secondary memory into the main memory for execution of the program. Then the control is transferred to that. There are various loading schemes available like absolute, relocating and direct linking. The loader also performs the linking functions. The linker links all the object modules of the program concerned and the necessary libraries. It is actually a part of a loader's function only. The Fig. 7.1 shows the organization of the loader. The function of the loader can be clearly understood from this Fig. 7.1.

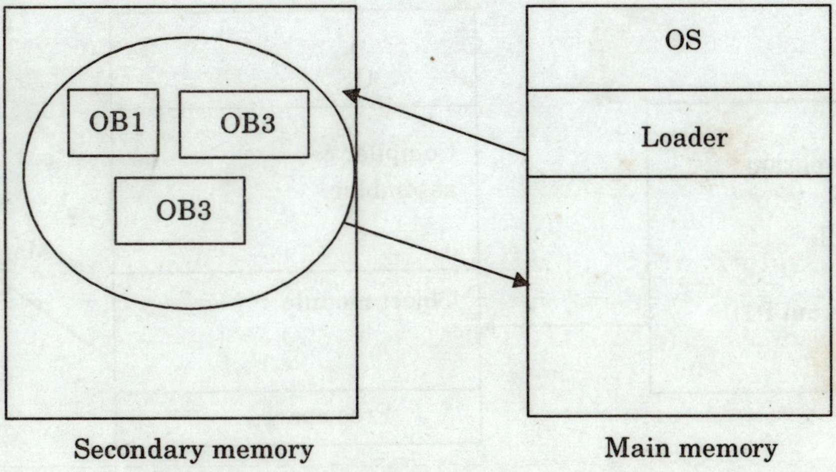

Fig. 7.1 Loader

In this figure, OB1, OB2 and OB3 are object modules. These are loaded from the secondary memory into the main memory. The loader resides in the main memory.

7.2 LOADERS

There are various loading schemes available and some of the important schemes are listed below:

1. Compile and go loaders
2. Absolute loaders
3. Relocating loaders and
4. Linking loaders

The functions and other details of these loaders are discussed in this section.

7.2.1 Compile and Go Loaders

Initially the loading was the function of the assembler only. In such assemblers the object programs are not stored in the secondary memory. The object programs are available in the main memory itself where the assembler is also available. When the object program is to be executed, the control is transferred to that part of the memory by the assembler. No loaders are necessary in this case. This type of loading is called as "compile and go" loading scheme (compile and go loaders). The Fig. 7.2 gives clear idea about the compile and go loading scheme. The program module in any HLL (High Level Language), say P1, undergoes translation through compiler and assemblers and the corresponding object module is stored directly in the main memory itself. The assembler is already residing in main memory. This loading scheme has some disadvantages. The assembler occupies more memory. Not only that every time the assembly process is to be done. This type loading will not support advanced features in the operating system like multi programming and multi tasking and others. If the program has subroutines it will be difficult to handle by these loading schemes. This necessiates a separate loading scheme. So only the loaders came into use.

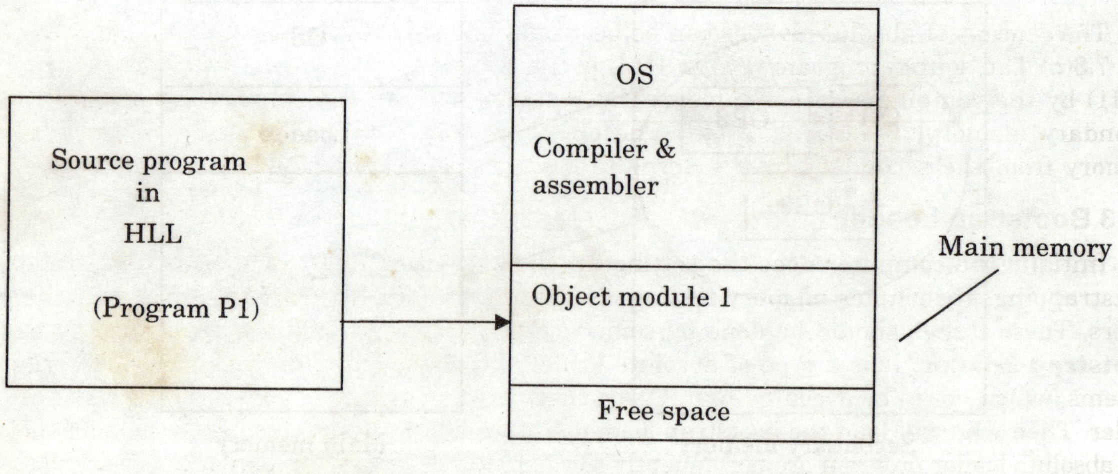

Fig. 7.2 Compile and Go Loading Scheme

7.2.2 Absolute Loader

The assembler places the object program directly in the secondary memory (cards or any other secondary memory devices), instead of loading in main memory. This loader loads the object program into the main memory for execution. The assembler will also generate the address information for the loader. The assembler will specify the address for placing the object program in the main memory. It is a simple type of loader. All the addresses for object modules for various programming modules and relocation addresses are generated by the assembler.

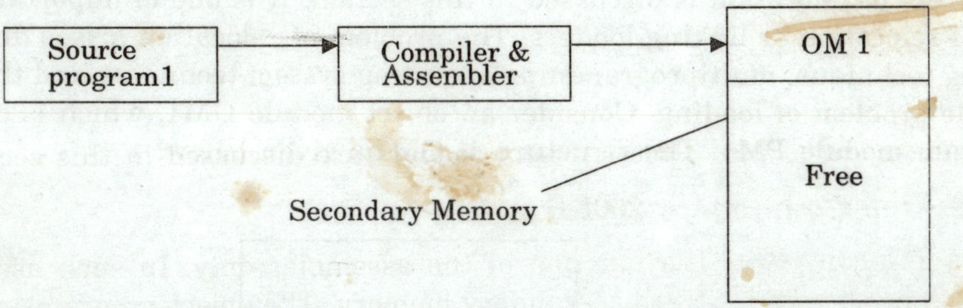

(*a*) Translation of the source program into object program

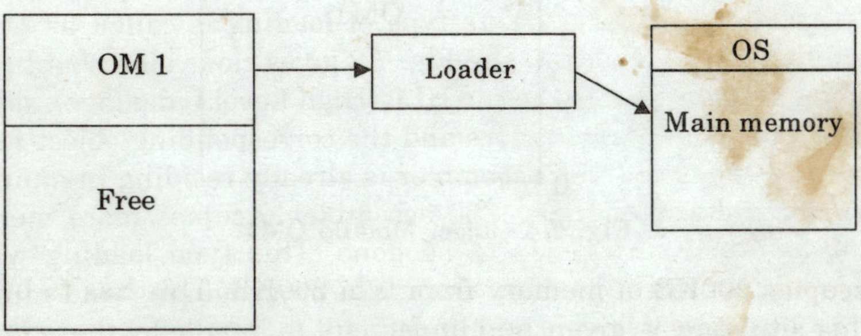

(*b*) Loading the object program into main memory

Fig. 7.3 Absolute loading scheme

The concept of absolute loader can be best understood with the help of the Figs. 7.3 (*a*) and 7.3(*b*) The source program (P1) in HLL is converted into corresponding object program (OM1) by the compiler and assemblers. The assembler places the object program into the secondary memory. Refer Fig. 7.3.(*a*) The object module (OM1) is loaded into the main memory from the secondary by the absolute loader. Refer Fig. 7.3.(*b*).

7.2.3 Bootstrap Loader

Initially the computer does the setting up work for carrying out the operations, called bootstrapping. It includes memory testing, devices testing, POST (Power On Self Test) and others. These things should be done by some routines and these routines are loaded by the **Bootstrap Loader.** It is a type of absolute loader, which loads the programs like operating systems, which are to be executed first. Okay, the operating system is loaded by the bootstrap loader. Then who will load the bootstrap loader? This has to be loaded first. In some machines this absolute loader program are permanently stored in ROM (Read Only Memory). On switching 'ON' the system, the computer executes this ROM program. There is lot of similar hardware dependent mechanisms available for executing the bootstrap loader.

7.2.4 Relocating Loaders

The loaders, which allow program relocation, are called relocating or relative loaders. The need for relocating loaders can be understood with the help of the figure shown in Fig. 7.4. There are some address sensitive subroutines and whose addresses will be changed sometimes. This leads to relocation of all the routines. The relocating loader solves this problem.

Relocation

The concept of relocation is discussed in this section. It is one of important concept for the design of relocation or linking loaders. The problem of relocation arises due to modular programming technique, multiprogramming operating system technique and the like. Let us take a simple problem of loading. Consider an object module OM1, which is corresponding to the program module PM1. The structure of OM1is given below:

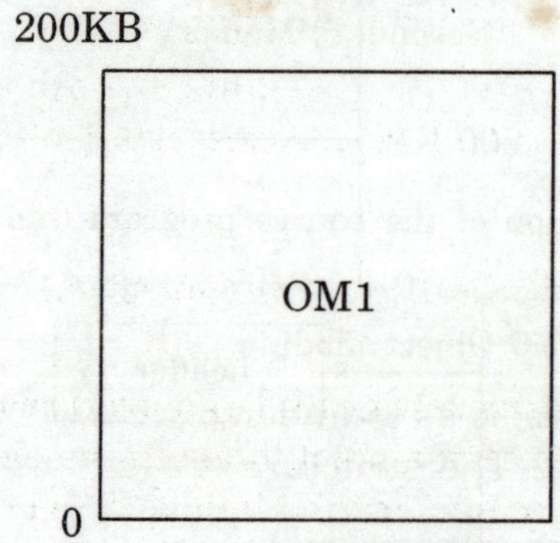

Fig. 7.4 Object Module OM1

This OM1 occupies 200KB of memory from 0 to 200KB. This has to be loaded into the main memory. This situation is given hereunder:

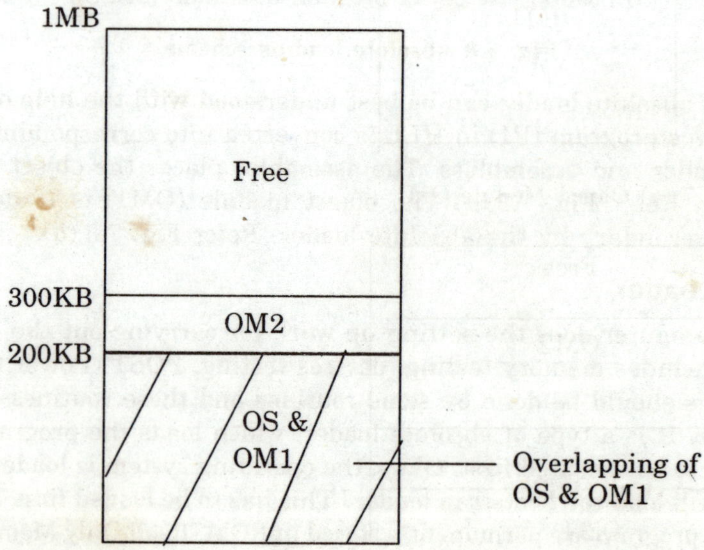

Fig. 7.5 Object module OM1 is placed in memory without relocation

In the main memory, already operating system occupies the memory from 0 to 200 KB. Now the object module 0M1 has to be placed over the operating system (*i.e.,*) from 200 KB onwards. But OM1 has been placed from 0 to 200 KB. Now there is an overlap, this leads to problems and confusions. The solution is relocation. The module OM1 has to be addressed from 200 KB to 400 KB. So the starting address of OM1 is 200. This is called relocation. The object module OM1's starting address is added with a relocation constant 200. The Fig. 7.6 gives the position of OM1 after relocation.

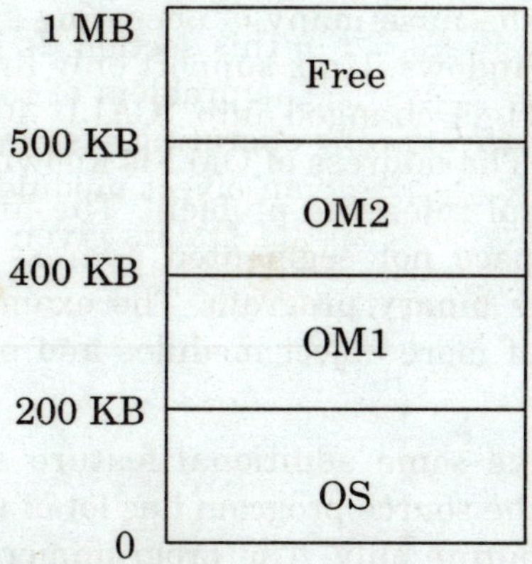

Fig. 7.6 Object module OM1 after relocation

Let us see another example so as to understand the concept of Relocation. Consider two object modules OM1 and OM2. The structure of OM1 and OM2 are given below.

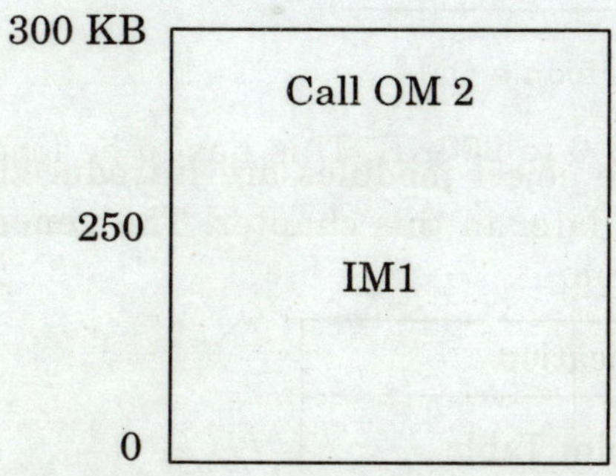

Fig. 7.7 (*a*) Object Module OM1

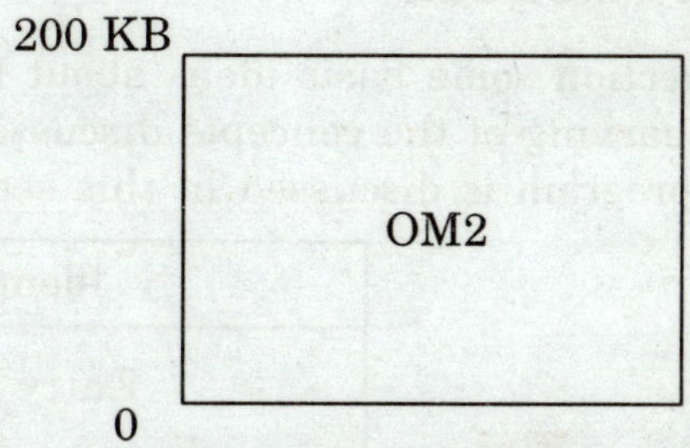

Fig. 7.7 (*b*) Object module OM2

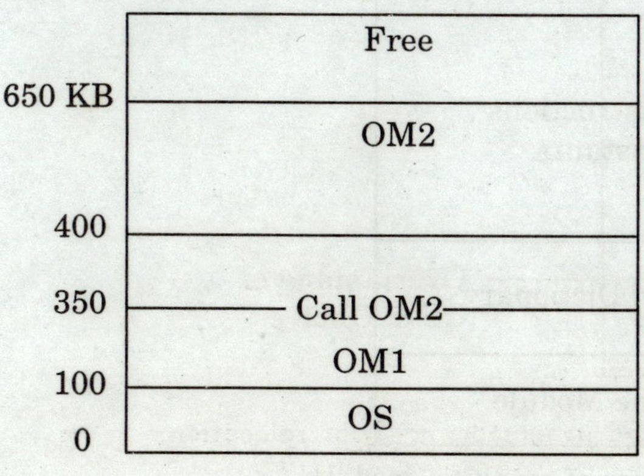

Fig. 7.7 (*c*) Before location

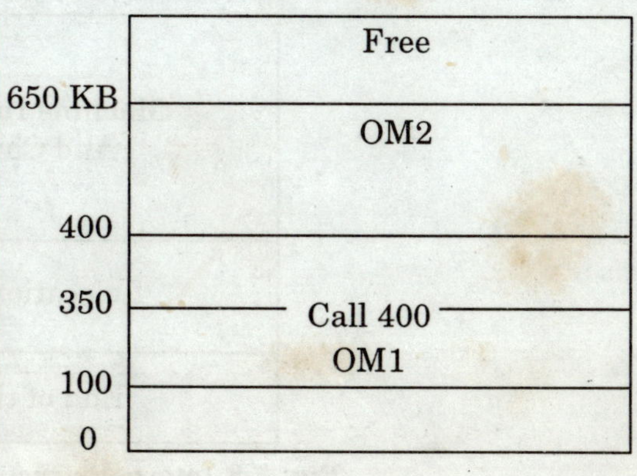

Fig. 7.7 (*d*) After relocation & linking

The OM1 and OM2 occupies 300 KB and 250 KB of memory. These two object modules have to be linked together and also here relocation has also to be done so as to create the executable binary program. The Figs. 7.7 (*a*), 7.7 (*b*) show the structure of OM1 and OM2. The OM1 has a calling statement. It calls the OM2. This refers the name of some other structure. This can be called as external reference.

The Figs. 7.7 (*c*), 7.7 (*d*) show how relocation and linking are done. The OM1 is shifted by 100 KB and OM2 is shifted by 400. This is to create a single linear address space for the modules to be executed. This is because many of operating systems support only the linear address space. All versions of Windows, Unix support only linear address space. The calling statement "CALL OM2" is OM1 is changed into "CALL 400", since after relocation and linking "OM2 is placed at 400". The address of OM2 is known only at the linking time. This problem can be called as external reference problem. The linked, relocated OM1 and OM2 occupy single linear address space not segmented address space. This is now ready for execution. This gives executable binary program. The example discussed is a simple one. The complication will increase if more object modules and external references are present in the source program.

The linking loader can have some additional feature so as to ease the operation of linking and loading. Generally the source program has lot of standard library functions. The library function is in fact subroutine only. The programmers encourage the use of library functions, so the linking loaders should include these subroutines from the library into the program. These routines are to be fetched from the library. This is necessary for all the subroutines under this category. This process can be done automatically. Then this called automatic library call.

7.3 OBJECT MODULE

In this section some basic ideas about the object modules are introduced, which will support the learning of the concepts discussed later in this chapter. The general structure of an object program is discussed in this section.

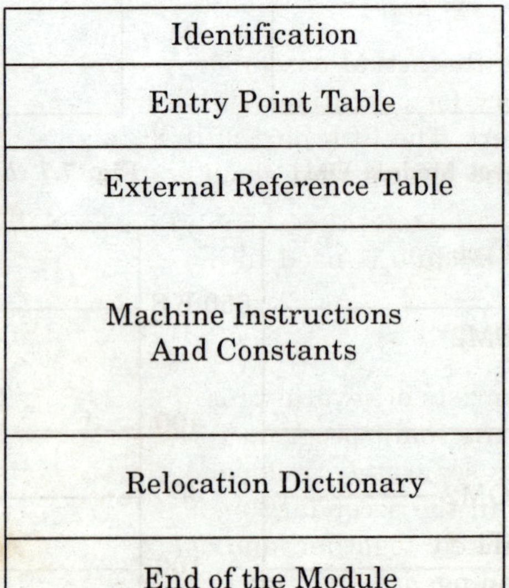

Fig. 7.8 Internal structure of an object module

The object modules have been very extensively discussed throughout the book. The object modules are the outcome of translators like compilers and assemblers. The compiler converts any program written in a HLL into an object program. The assembler converts any program written in assembly language program into an object program. (The assembler works as a part of the complier for translating the HLL program, and also works independently for converting the assembly language program). There will be object modules corresponding to the program modules in the source program.

The structure of any object module generally consists of the following parts.

1. Identification
2. Entry point table
3. External reference table
4. Machine instructions and constants
5. Relocation dictionary and
6. End of module.

These parts constitute the internal structure of any object module. The 'identification' part keeps the name of the object module.

The second part is entry point table. This table keeps the list of symbols, which are defined in this module, and also can be referenced by other modules. Their corresponding addresses are also maintained here. E.g., say, symbol 1 is defined inside the object module. Then the name symbol 1 and its address will be maintained in this table. The programmers using the pseudo-instructions "PUBLIC" will indicate the contents of the entry point table in the assembly language program.

The third part of the object module is "External reference table". This table maintains the details of the symbols, which are referenced in this module but defined in some other modules. The instructions, which use these symbols, will also be maintained here. This will be useful during insertion of correct addresses of these external symbols. The symbols are declared as external using the pseudo instruction "EXTERN" in the assembly language program.

The fourth part will be the actual assembler code and data. This is the part will be loaded into the main memory for execution. The remaining parts of the object module are used by the linker and loaders. The fifth part of the Object module is relocation dictionary. This dictionary maintains the information about the address to be relocated. This will be useful during relocation.

The last part is end of module is used to indicate the end of the object module.

7.4 LINKING LOADERS

Generally a program consists of several procedures. We can also say a program is a set of procedures. Some times the main program itself treated as a procedure. The compiler translates all the procedures separately, independently into distinct object modules. These are most of the time stored in the secondary memory (disk). In order to execute the object modules, these must be linked together and loaded into main memory. Now we can understand linking and loading are the functions necessary for executing the program. Linking of various object modules are done by the linker. The linker is actually part of loader only. The linker's function is to collect various object modules and link them together called as 'Executable binary Program'. This can be treated as a single entity. Linker links necessary libraries for the execution of a program, during the execution.

In MS DOS, Windows the object files are having the extension **'.obj'** and the executable program has the extension **'.exe'.** In unix environment the object files have the extension **'.o'**, and the executable binary program has no extension. The loader can be a linking loader if it is linking the necessary libraries and symbolic references. It is actually part of loader only. It does also relocating. These receive set of object program modules as input to be linked together. It eliminates the disadvantages of other loading schemes. It also takes care of relocation. It allows the use of multiple modules, segments, and routines in a user program. It also allows for referencing the symbols from all the modules and segments.

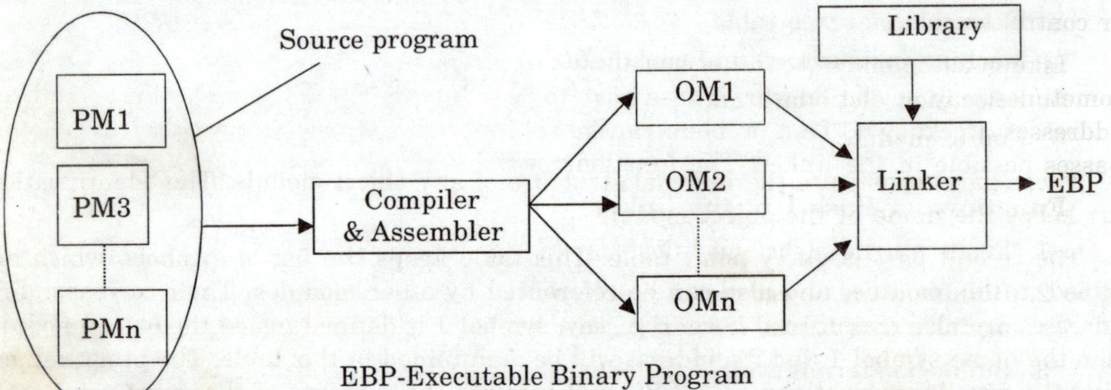

Fig. 7.9 Linker

In Fig. 7.9 an example source program is considered. It uses modular programming. There are 'n' modules (may be subroutines or procedures) namely PM1, PM2, and up to PMn. These are converted into corresponding object modules OM1, OM2... OMn, by the translators compiler and assemblers. The object modules OM1, OM2... OMn, are given as inputs to the linker. The linker takes the necessary library functions as another input. All the object modules and the necessary libraries are linked together by the linker program. The output of the linker is Executable Binary Program (EBP).

7.4.1 Design of a Linking Loader

The linker links the separate address spaces of the object modules into a single linear address space. This is the major function of the linker. The linker receives the object modules as input and links them together for execution. The linker constructs a table called **Object Module Table** for maintaining the details about the various object modules. This table is helpful in linking the object modules. This table maintains the details about the object modules like name, memory capacity and the pointer (starting address) to the corresponding object modules. The following Fig. 7.10 gives an idea about the object module table.

Name of the object module	*Pointer*	*Memory capacity*
Prod 1	1100	300
Prod 2	1400	700
...	...	...
Prod n	400	500

Fig. 7.10 Object modules table

The linker assigns the starting address to each module based on the pointer details available in the object module table. This relocation is necessary because some memory space is allocated for the operating system routines in the main memory. We can understand why relocation is necessary from the discussions of the previous section. The linker adds the relocation constant for every memory reference instructions equal to the starting address of every module. This is done in order to solve the relocation problem. This is also addressed in the previous section. The linker identifies the instructions, which refer the other procedures (control sections) and attaches the addresses of the respective procedures. It resolves external references too. Referring an external symbol can be called as external reference. If a symbol is referenced within a particular subroutine (sometimes called as control sections), then it is called internal reference. External symbol is a symbol defined in a different subroutine or control section.

Like in assemblers the linker has also two passes. The addresses of the external symbol sometimes may not be known. These have to be resolved. These cannot be linked until the addresses are known. This problem can be resolved by introducing passes. There are two passes possible in the linker. The functions of the two passes are given hereunder.

Functions of Pass 1 of the linker

1. Reads all the object modules.
2. Builds up the object module table, which maintains about the details of the object modules like name, memory used and starting address.
3. Builds a external symbol table, which consisting of external symbols, which can be used globally.
4. Assigns addresses to all the external symbols to resolve the external reference problem.

Functions of Pass 2 of the linker

1. Reads the object modules, relocates and links one module at a time, to create an executable binary program. It performs actual loading, relocation and linking.

Linking can be done in two ways as listed below:

1. Using linkage editors
2. Dynamic linking

7.5 LINKAGE EDITORS

In linkage editors, linking is done before load time. There is a separate editor, which performs all the linking operations. The output of the linking editor can be directly loaded into the main memory for execution. It performs linking and some relocation. The linked program is written to a file or library instead of being immediately loaded into the memory. This approach reduces the overhead when the program is executed. Only relocation is necessary at load time.

It is an editor, which is used to do the linking operation before the load time. This is a separate editor it does all the operation of a linker before the load time, not at the runtime. The linkage editor receives the various object modules and some library function as input. It does the linking of the object modules and the libraries as a linker. This is not directly loaded into the main memory. Instead this linked program is stored in a file or library. This can be used whenever necessary. If a program is to be repeatedly executed, this method will yield very good results. This eliminates the linking operation every time. Time is greatly reduced. Overhead is also reduced when the program is executed.

The difference between the linkage editor and linker can be listed below

Table 7.1. Comparison between linker and linkage editor

Linker	Linkage Editor
1. Linking of object modules and necessary libraries are done and immediately loaded into main memory.	1. Linking of object modules and necessary libraries are done and stored in a file or library. The o/p is called linked program
2. Only once it can be used.	2. Many number of times it can be used as necessity arises
3. Library search and resolution of external reference must be done each time once.	3. Library search and resolution of external reference must be done only once.
4. This type of linking is not suitable for program, which is executed repeatedly.	4. This is very much suitable for program, which is executed repeatedly.

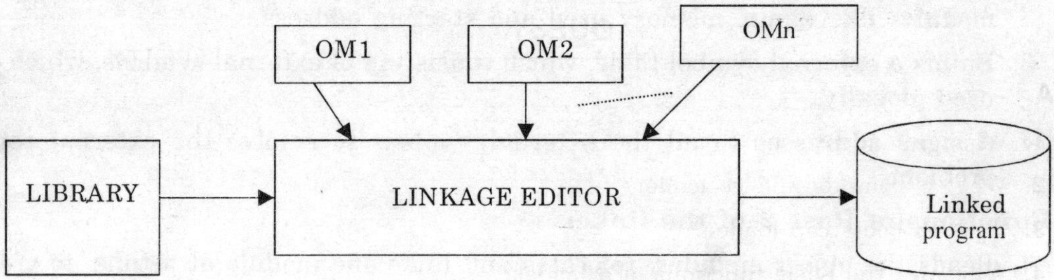

Fig. 7.11 Linkage editor

The Fig. 7.11 gives clear idea about the linkage editor. The object modules OM1, OM2.....OMn are given as inputs to the linkage editor along with the necessary library functions. The linkage editor does the linking of all the object modules (0M1 to OMn) and the necessary library functions. The linkage editor also solves the problem of external references. The linked program, which will be output of the linkage editor, is stored in a file or library. This can be loaded into the main memory whenever necessary for execution. The linked program is more suitable for relocating loaders. This is given to the relocating loader. The loader does the relocation and the linked program becomes ready for execution. The linked program is also as load image.

7.6 DYNAMIC LINKING

In dynamic linking, linking of any subroutine is done at the time (run time) when it is first called. It has extra overhead than the linking loader. The dynamic linking arises due to the advent of advanced hardware and operating system features. Especially in multi programming OS technique, some modules will be swapped-in and some modules will be swapped-out due to its preemptive nature. So some modules only will be available in the main memory for execution. All the modules are not necessary at a particular time for execution. The needed modules alone will be linked and loaded into the main memory.

If the program to be executed is larger in size than the memory available in the system, then all of its modules can't be together loaded into the main memory. So the program is divided into segments or pages. Only needed segments or pages will alone be linked into the main memory. After the execution of these segments or pages, another set of segments or pages will be linked and loaded into the main memory. This is called dynamic linking and loading. Sometimes in the other loading (static) schemes, some modules, which are linked and loaded into the main memory, will never be used. This leads to wastage of overhead. But in dynamic linking and loading scheme, this disadvantage is eliminated. The modules needed for the execution will alone be linked and loaded into the main memory.

Summary

In this chapter the basic concepts of loading and linking are introduced and discussed in detail. The general structure of an object module is discussed here. The various loading schemes are discussed in a very simple style. The concepts of relocation and linking are discussed with examples. The linkage editor, which does the linking process in advance, is also discussed. This in fact helps the linker. The concepts of dynamic linking are also discussed in the end.

QUESTIONS

Part A

1. What is loader?
2. What is compile and go loader?
3. What is bootstrap loader?
4. What are the basic functions of a loader?
5. What do you mean by program relocation?
6. What is known as absolute loader?
7. What are the steps involved in the execution of a program?
8. What is a binary program?
9. What does the object module for a program consist of?
10. What do you mean by program relocation?
11. What do you mean by linking?
12. What is meant by non-relocatable program?
13. What do you mean by self relocatable program?
14. What are the basic categories of information that an object module contains?
15. What is the function of a linker?
16. What are the functions performed by two pass linker?
17. Name the data structures constructed in the two passes of linker and list its contents.
18. What is relocatable program?
19. What the differences between linkage editor and linker?

20. What is dynamic linking?
21. What are the functions of two pass loader?

Part B

1. Briefly explain the functions of bootstrap loader.
2. Explain in detail about the basic functions of a loader with examples.
3. What is the need for a loader? Compare the following loaders:
   (*i*) Absolute loader
   (*ii*) Bootstrap loader
   (*iii*) Linking loader
4. What is linkage editor? Give the functions of the same
5. Explain the design of a loader with an example.
6. Explain various loading schemes available and compare the advantages and disadvantages.
7. Explain the design of a two pass loader? Give also brief note on the data structures used in the construction of the same.
8. What is a load image? What the ways to get the load image of a program? Explain.

CHAPTER 8

INTERPRETERS, EDITORS AND DEBUGGERS

Blessed are those who are persecuted for righteousness' sake,
For theirs is the kingdom of heaven.

8.1 INTERPRETERS

8.1.1 Introduction

Interpreter is special type of system program. It is a translator similar to compiler, which converts the source program written in any high level language into object program by interpreting the source program instructions. We will discuss about the two types of control units called hardwired and micro programmed control units. The concepts behind these control units will help the reader to understand the function of an interpreter. A list of definitions is also given in this chapter. This chapter gives the design concepts of an interpreter also. A brief note on the Java programming language is given under the heading "Java—An interpreted language", which addresses about the interpretation aspects of Java.

8.1.2 RISC and CISC Machines

There are two types of computers based on the instruction set they have. They are listed below:

1. Reduced Instruction Set Computers (RISC machines)
2. Complex Instruction Set Computers (CISC machines)

The control unit of the computer generates timing and control signals for execution of instructions. The control units can be either hardwired control unit or micro programmed control unit. The hard-wired control unit is constructed using combinational and sequential circuits. They use flip-flops, decoders and other hardwired (hardware) circuits. The control signals are generated by this hard-wired circuitry. In case of micro programmed control unit the control signals are generated by the micro programs, which are residing in the control memory of this control unit. A micro program is a set of microinstructions. A micro program is written for a particular instruction in the instruction set of the computer. This micro program is responsible for generating the control signals in this control unit. In the micro programmed control unit the control signals are generated by software not by a hardware circuit.

The Reduced Instruction Set Computers (RISC) has the hardwired control units generally. They use compilers for translating the source program into the corresponding object program.

The Complex Instruction Set Computers (CISC) has the micro programmed control units normally. They use the interpreters for converting the source program into the corresponding object codes by interpreting the source program instructions. For each the source program instruction, there will be one or more assembly language instructions based on the instruction set of that machine. For every assembly language instruction, there will be a micro program available in the control memory of the micro programmed control unit. This micro program will generate the control signals. This process is called interpreting. Here for every source program instruction, there will be a micro program invoked. This will immediately generate the control signals. That is why we say interpreter converts the source program line by line. And the errors also, after every source program instruction, are indicated.

BASIC, Tcl, PERL, Java are some examples for interpreted languages. Java language has the unique feature of using the compilers and interpreters. The Java compiler creates the byte code version of the source program. The Java byte code is the intermediate version of the source program. These byte codes will be interpreted by the Java interpreter and executed. The java byte codes cannot be directly executed. The Java Virtual Machine (JVM) does interpretation of the byte code. Because of this unique feature Java programs can be run on any machine, which has java virtual machine. That is why Java is platform independent and architecturally neutral. We say, 'Write once, Run everywhere', for a Java program because of this unique feature only.

Compilers and interpreters can be used in both the RISC and CISC machines. The choice can be dependent on the situation and application.

8.1.3 Interpreters

There are lot of definitions available for the interpreter. We will see some definitions of the interpreter which given hereunder. These definitions will give an idea about interpreters and its functions. The comparision of interpreters with compilers are also given here.

Interpreter takes the HLL program as input and examines each instruction in turn and executes the equivalent sequence of microinstructions. It does not generate the machine language program. This process is called as interpretation. The compiler generates the machine language program corresponds to the HLL source program.

In interpretation each HLL instruction is examined and decoded and executed immediately. No translated program is generated. The interpreter is in control of the computer.

The compiler is a translator, which converts the HLL program into an equivalent program in machine language. The computer then executes the machine language program instead of the HLL program. The computer controls the compiler.

An interpreter takes a string of characters called pseudo code and converts it into actual code that is then executed. The interpreter is software (machine) that interprets pseudo code in a way that makes it executable. It interprets the programs written in programming languages. It can interpret any kind of encoding into a usable form.

An interpreter processes a source program written in a HLL, just like the compiler. But the interpreter executes a version of the source program, instead of translating it into machine code.

It is also a translator like compiler. It translates a HLL program into object codes, statement wise. It does not translate the entire program at a time. It takes up one statement of HLL program at a time translates it and then executes it. Then it takes the next statement of the HLL program and does the same process.

A program that fetches, examines and executes the instructions of another program is called as an interpreter.

An interpreter is a program that appears to execute a source program as if it were machine language program.

An interpreter occupies less memory space; it is cheaper, and suitable for smaller system. It is slower than a compiler. Interpreters have quick turn-around time, which is useful for interactive systems. There is no edit, compile and test cycle. They are portable.

8.1.4 Design of an Interpreter

Interpretation

In this section we are going to discuss about the interpretation technique. This section discusses about the components involved in the interpretation process.

The interpretation can be done in two ways. In the first way, the source code is taken and the corresponding executable codes are generated. Here there is no preprocessing done. The source program is taken as such. Such type of interpretation is permitted in interpreter base systems. In this case the source program is kept as such. The overhead is more in these systems.

In the second way, some type of preprocessing is done. The source program is converted into an **intermediate representation** after preprocessing. This intermediate representation is used for interpretation. The overhead is comparatively less in this type of interpretation. The speed of interpretation is increased due to the use of intermediate representation.

The interpretation process has three major components. They are listed below:

1. Micro programs
2. Symbol table and
3. Data store.

The input and output of an interpreter are given below:

Input: Source program in HLL

Output: Executable machine code

We will discuss each component listed above, in this section.

Microprograms

Consider an executable statement in the source program to be interpreted. This statement is decoded for identifying the actual operation of it. The interpreter systems run on micro-programmed control units. In the micro programmed control units there will be control memory present. The control memory keeps the micro programs, which correspond to the executable statements in the source program. A micro program is a set of microinstructions to carrying out a computation. After decoding the meaning of the source program statement, the corresponding the micro program will be invoked. This microprogram will generate the control signals. The control signals are responsible for execution. The control signals are software controlled. This is how the source program is interpreted.

Symbol Table

The symbol table maintains the details of the symbols present in the source program. The symbols are identifier names, labels or name of any program segments. The attributes of the symbols are maintained in the symbol table. The names of the key words are also maintained in the symbol tables. There is lot of data structures available for symbol tables. The concepts of symbol tables are addressed in detail in the chapters 4 and 5. The readers can refer these for more details.

Data Store

The data store keeps the necessary data items for variables, identifiers and others. There are various distinct data types present and are used during interpretation of the source program.

8.1.5 Java—An Interpreted Language

Java is a unique type of language that is an interpreted language. Java language source program can be executed using both the compilers and interpreters. This section discusses about the unique features of Java programming language. The discussion concentrates mainly on the aspects interpretation part of Java interpreter.

The Java is completely object oriented programming language. It is architecturally neutral. Java is platform independent. A Java program can be executed anywhere. That is why is called 'Write once, run everywhere' type of programming language.

Consider a Java program and it is submitted to Java compiler. The output of Java compiler is non executable code. It is called byte code. Byte code is a highly optimized set of instructions designed to be executed by the Java run time system. The Java run time system is nothing but Java Virtual Machine (JVM). The Java virtual machine is an interpreter for byte code. Most of the modern languages are designed to be compiled not interpreted. The Java program is interpreted and executed by the JVM. The byte code is capable of being executed in a wide variety of environments. The reason is JVM is implemented in each platform. The details of JVM differ from platform to platform; all interpret the same byte code. If a Java program were compiled to native code (Based on the architecture of machine it runs), then different versions of the same program would have to exist for each type processor connected to the Internet. Interpretation of byte code is the easiest way to create truly portable programs. The concept of interpretation makes the Java program secure.

If a program is interpreted it generally runs substantially slower than it would run if compiled to executable code. The JVM is considerably faster. We can conclude like this.

Java enables the creation of cross-platform programs by compiling into an intermediate representation called Java byte code. This byte code can be interpreted on any system that provides a Java virtual machine.

In Java, a source file is called a compilation unit. Java compiler requires that a source file use **". java"**, extension. For example, "demo. java". The java compiler **'javac'** creates a file called "demo. class", which contains the byte code version of the program. The java byte code is the intermediate representation of the source program that has the instructions, which can be executed by Java interpreter. The output of "javac" is not the code that can be directly executed. In order to run the program, Java interpreter uses the command as given below:

"java demo"

The block diagram shown below (Fig. 8.1) gives the clear idea about the processes in Java compilation and interpretation.

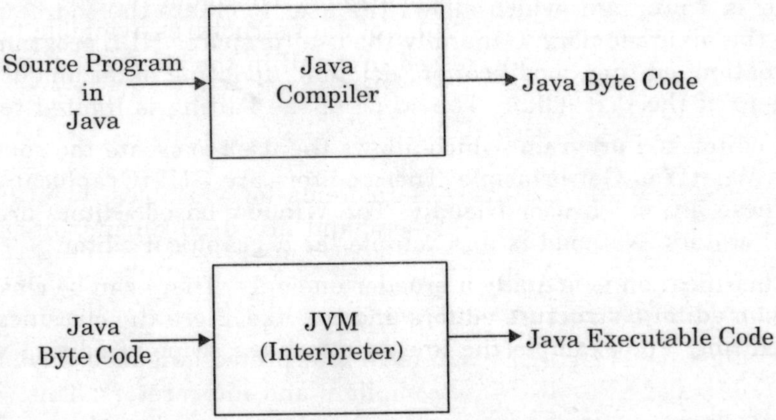

Fig. 8.1 Java compiler and Interpreter

8.2. EDITORS

This section discusses about the software development tools. These tools actually support software development. In this section we will see about the basic concepts of Editors and Debuggers. What are the design concepts involved for the design of editors and debuggers? These are all addressed in this section. Some example for editors and debuggers and their features are also discussed in this section. The section 8.2.1 discusses about the editors and the section 8.3 discusses about the debuggers.

8.2.1 Editors

The system program editors and debuggers will help for the development of system program and other programs. These are like word processors. Some examples for editors are Turbo C editor, Vi editor, Borland C editor and others. These are program development tools. Editors are basically software development tools. They support the creation and modification of documents. The editor is a program, which allows creating a file, which can contain C program, C++ program, assembly language program and the like. It also allows modifying, updating of the files. These are all word processing software.

If a file is created in an editor, ASCII codes for all the letters, numbers and characters are stored in the main memory by the editor. The file is created in the main memory **(RAM)** only. When it is completed, the file is stored in the secondary memory either in the floppy disk or in hard disk with the corresponding extension. Example: Let us say, we create a C program file in the Turbo C editor. As we create the file the, for each character in the file the corresponding ASCII code is stored in the main memory. When we want store (by giving save option) then the file it will be stored in the secondary memory like hard disk with the extension ".c " as in a file name 'sys.c'. As we progress the editor will assist in the development of the file. For example in the MS WORD, we get assistance for spell checking, grammatical error correction and others.

The editors may be classified into two types as given below:

1. Textual editors
2. Graphical editors

A text editor is a program, which allows the user to create the source program in the form of text into the main memory. Generally the user prepares HLL program or any source program. The creation, editing, modification, deletion, updating of document or files can be done with the help of the text editor. The scope of the editing is limited to the text only.

A graphical editor is a program, which allows the user to create the source program in What You See Is What You Get principle. These editors are GUI (Graphical User Interface) based editors. These are much user friendly. The Window based editors are best example for the graphical editors. Notepad is an example for a graphical editor.

The above classification is actually a broader one only. There can be classifications like line editors, stream editors, structure editors and the like. Here the classification is limited to the scope of editing. For example the line editors have scope of editing with respect of line of text only.

8.2.2 Design of an Editor

In this section we are going to see the design of an editor. The basic operations of an editor and the design concepts are addressed in this section.

There are various functions, which are supposed to be performed by an editor. The name itself implies that the major function of an editor is editing. Apart from editing, the editor has to do other supporting services to editing. The editors are word processors. (There is lot of word processors available. The simplest one is word star. Some word processors can convert a given story to a screenplay.

The major functions of an editor are editing, traveling, viewing, and displaying. The most important function is the creation of files. A file is a group of characters defined by its creator. The creator may define a file as a program file or a database file or a document file and the like. Creation of a file is to be done first then only the above said operations can be performed. The editor must allow the user to create a file of his interest.

Editing means modifying, updating, deleting and formatting of the text. Traveling means the ability to travel the text in the file. This allows the user to move the cursor over the text. Viewing option allows the user to create a view of the file. This involves selection of font, style, colors and the like. This view created can be called as abstract view.

Displaying and printing is another function of the editor. The editor should generate the printable view. This is to display on the screen. This is conversion of abstract view into physical view. The printers should also print this.

The editors should provide facilities for all the above mentioned functions.

There are many other advanced features like spell checking and grammar checking as the document is being created. The editors can have the facilities for the editing the image and pictures.

The editors can be developed using C, C++, VB, VC++ programming tools. There are plenty of commercial editors available in the market.

8.3 DEBUGGERS

A debugger is also a program, which allows debugging, trouble shooting any program. It allows the user to run the program in steps. *i.e.* statement by statement we can execute the program. This allows us to trace the program to find where exactly the error is. For example, in Borland C we can debug using the options available for debugging and tracing. The key **"F7"** is used to execute the program, statement by statement. The key **"F8"** is used to run the program, procedure by procedure. The key **"Ctrl F7"** helps the user to watch any variable. With this feature the user can watch the value of the variable, its address, and intermediate values of the variable at every execution. This really helps to debugging *i.e.* in error correcting.

(In those days mechanical computers were used. They employed livers, pulleys, wheels and other mechanical components. In those times, sometimes bugs (insects) got into the mechanical components. This resulted in erroneous results. When the bugs are removed the errors were corrected. Hence "Removing bugs" was called as **Debugging**. Still that name is used for error correction. This is the history for the word debugging.)

Debugger is a program, which allows the user to test and debug the programs. All computers provide the debugging facility. A program can be tested in single steps (step by step). It allows executing and testing every step of the program. The user can see and examine the contents of the registers and memory locations after execution of every computation. The debugger also provides facility to set break points in the program and test the program.

The debuggers should give the following facilities:

1. Allowing to put breakpoints in the program
2. Start a debug dialog when the control reaches a break point
3. Displaying the details of program entities being debugged
4. Giving values to program entities
5. Testing user defined assertions and predicates

The process of finding and removing errors in the program is called debugging.

The debugging is generally done in two ways. They are

1. Single step control and
2. Break point method.

8.3.1 Single Step Control

In this method the user can execute the program in steps. After executing each step, the user can check contents of the registers, memory (by specifying some address) and variables. This will help in finding the errors and eliminating them also.

In Borland C, we have debugging options available. The key **'F7'** is used to execute the program in steps. There is one more option available, which is used to watch the expression. This can be done using the '**ctrl F7**' key pair. If a user wants to know the value of a variable say 'a', then he must first select the F7 option to run the program in steps. Then he has to press **ctrl F7,** then, "watch window" will be displayed. The user has to type the variable 'a' in the add watch window. Then the value of 'a' will be displayed in the watch window. If '&a' is given as expression then the address of a will be displayed in the watch window. The user can directly place the cursor under the variable a in the program and press **ctrl F7,** then also the same thing will happen. The key '**F8**' is used to run the program in procedure wise. In case of programs in larger size, the method of running in steps will be time consuming and tedious. If one procedure is checked we need not check it again. But in running in steps method, this has to be rechecked, though it is done already. The method of running in procedure wise solves this problem. We can directly execute a procedure by pressing F8 key. We can run the procedure in steps after selecting a particular procedure using the key F8. This is a simple example for debugging process for a C++ program. Similarly in other programming languages and tools debugging can be done.

The method of running in steps is very slow. This method is more time consuming. This method may not be suitable for larger programs. This method cannot find timing errors and errors in DMA (Direct Memory Access).

8.3.2 Break Point Method

The break point method, as the name implies allows the user to set break points in the program in order to check the contents of the registers, memory and other programming entities like variables. In fact the break point allows the user to halt the execution of the program at that break point. Then the user can examine the intermediate results of the program execution. The user can then examine the contents of the registers, variables, addresses and I/O ports. The break point can be introduced at any point in the program by the user.

In Intel 8085 processor consider the following instruction:

"RST n"

This instruction is software interrupt to the processor. This is used to restart the execution at the specified point. Here 'n' varies from 0 to 8. RST is INTR instruction. There can be up to 8 interrupt instructions. This means that there can be up to 8 I/O devices connected to INTR through external hardware.

This method is faster. Testing and debugging a loop is very difficult in case of single step control. The break point method can be used for debugging the loops. The programmer can set a break point at any point in the program in this method. The program will run in the normal speed till reaches the break point and then it stops. Then the programmer can debug that area of the code. This allows the programmer to localize the error and also allows the programmer to skip the code which is error free. Generally the break point method does not affect the timing of the program. So it can be used to check input, output and errors.

Example 8.1

Label	Mnemonics	Operands	Comments
	MVI	C, FF	Move FF in register C
LOOP	DCR	C	Decrement register C
	JNZ	LOOP	Jump to LOOP if C is not zero
	RST	5	*Break Point*
	MVI	A, 04	Move 04 to accumulator
	STA	4500H	Store o4 in the accumulator
	HLT	76	Halt the execution

This is a simple 8085 program using a loop. This is program has break point after the execution of the loop. After the execution of the loop the programmer can check the contents of the program at various addresses. The generally used microprocessor kit can be used. It allows the programmer to check the program contents at runtime. The kit will be used to check by pressing "SI" key and next address key.

The example program is 8085 program. There are so many commercial compilers available. They can also be used in a similar way. All the commercial compilers like Turbo C, Borland C offers such facilities.

In the practical situations both the debugging methods are used separately or in combination. The break point method followed by the single step control provides better results in localizing the errors.

Summary

In this chapter the concepts of interpreters, editors and debuggers are discussed clearly. The design concepts of the interpreters are discussed in the chapter. An example for the interpreted language is also discussed in this chapter. The concepts with respect to interpretation of Java are addressed. In the next section the basic and design concepts of editors and debuggers are addressed in this chapter. The debugging methods are explained with some simple examples.

QUESTIONS

Part A

1. What is interpreter?
2. Define interpretation.
3. What are the differences between compilers and interpreters?
4. How RISC and CISC are relevant to interpretation?
5. Name few interpreted languages.
6. What is a micro program?
7. What is editor?
8. What the functions of an editor?
9. Name few popular editors.
10. What is a debugger?
11. What are the methods available for debugging?
12. What is dynamic debugging?

Part B

1. Explain the design of an interpreter in detail.
2. Discuss in detail about an editor and the design of an editor.
3. Discuss in detail about the debuggers in detail.
4. Discuss about the language features of Java with respect to interpretation.
5. Discuss about the debugging facilities in Turbo C and Turbo Pascal compilers.
6. Write note on:
   - *(i)* Windows based editors
   - *(ii)* Linux based editors
   - *(iii)* Image editing tools
7. Compare compilers and Interpreters.

APPENDIX

This appendix gives coding of a Two-pass assembler. This is developed in C++ language. This is implemented for assembly language programs written in Intel 8085 instruction set.

Input File

```
#include<fstream.h>
#include<conio.h>
#include<stdlib.h>
#include<stdio.h>
#include<ctype.h>
class refer_data
{
 private :
      char mne[20],data[20],lbel[15];

 public :
      void entry();
      void display();
};

main()
{
clrscr();
refer_data s;

ofstream wr;
```

```
ifstream rd;

wr.open("forref2.dat",ios :: app);

if(wr.fail())
{
cerr<<"File creation error";
exit(1);
}

char con;

do
{
s.entry();

wr.write((char *) &s,sizeof(s));

cout<<"\n Continue (y/n)";
con=getche();
}while(tolower(con)=='y');

wr.close();

rd.open("forref2.dat",ios :: in);

if(rd.fail())
{
cerr<<"File Open Error";
exit(1);
}

while(rd.read((char *) &s,sizeof(s)))
{
s.display();
}
rd.close();
```

```
getch();
}

void refer_data :: entry()
{
clrscr();
cout<<"Enter The Mne-Code";
fflush(stdin);
gets(mne);
cout<<"Enter The Data";
fflush(stdin);
gets(data);
cout<<"Enter Label";
fflush(stdin);
gets(lbel);
}

void refer_data :: display()
{
cout<<"\n";
cout<<"\n Mne-Code  : "<<mne;
cout<<"\n Data      : "<<data;
cout<<"\n lbel      : "<<lbel;
}
```

Mnemonics Table File

```
#include<fstream.h>
#include<conio.h>
#include<stdlib.h>
#include<stdio.h>
#include<ctype.h>
class table_data
{
 private :
      char mne[20],data[20],opcode[20];
      int len;
```

```
public :
        void entry();
        void display();
};

main()
{
clrscr();

table_data p;

ofstream wr;
ifstream rd;

wr.open("reftbl2.dat",ios :: app);

if(wr.fail())
{
cerr<<"File creation error";
exit(1);
}

char con;

do
{
p.entry();

wr.write((char *) &p,sizeof(p));

cout<<"\n Continue (y/n)";
con=getche();
}while(tolower(con)=='y');

wr.close();

rd.open("reftbl2.dat",ios :: in);
```

```
if(rd.fail())
{
cerr<<"File Open Error";
exit(1);
}

while(rd.read((char *) &p,sizeof(p)))
{
p.display();
}
rd.close();

getch();
}
void table_data :: entry()
{
clrscr();
cout<<"Enter The Mne-Code";
fflush(stdin);
gets(mne);
cout<<"Enter The Data";
fflush(stdin);
gets(data);
cout<<"Enter The Op_code";
fflush(stdin);
gets(opcode);
cout<<"Enter Length";
cin>>len;
}
void table_data :: display()
{
cout<<"\n";
cout<<"\n Mne-Code  : "<<mne;
cout<<"\n Data      : "<<data;
cout<<"\n Op_code   : "<<opcode;
cout<<"\n Length    : "<<len;
}
```

Comparison for forward references

```
#include<fstream.h>
#include<conio.h>
#include<stdlib.h>
#include<stdio.h>
#include<string.h>

class outfile_data
{
 private :
        long int lcode;
        char mne[20];
        char loc[15];
        char lbel[15];

 public :
        outfile_data();
        friend void compare1();
        friend void compare2();
        void display();
};


class refer_data
{
 private :
        char mne[20],data[20],lbel[15];

 public :
        friend void compare1();
        friend void compare2();
};


class table_data
{
```

```
private :
      char mne[20],data[20],opcode[20];
      int len;

public :
      friend void compare1();
      friend void compare2();
};

int tno=1;

main()
{
clrscr();
void compare1();
void compare2();


ofstream wr1;

ifstream rd1;
ifstream rd2;
ifstream rd3;

if(wr1.fail())
{
cerr<<"File creation error";
exit(1);
}

char con;

cout<<"\n Table Data";
cout<<"\n ===========";
cout<<"\n";
compare1();
cout<<"\n";
```

```
cout<<"\n";
cout<<"\n";
cout<<"\n Symbol Table";
cout<<"\n ============";
cout<<"\n";

compare2();

getch();
}

outfile_data :: outfile_data()
{
lcode=8000;
}

void compare1()
{
ifstream rd1;
ifstream rd2;
ofstream wr1;
outfile_data f;
refer_data d;
table_data t;

wr1.close();
 rd1.open("forref.dat",ios :: in);
 if(rd1.fail())
 {
 cout<<"\n File Open Error";
 exit(1);
 }
/* if(rd2.fail())
 {
 cout<<"\n File Open Error";
 exit(1);
 } */
```

```
wr1.open("forout1.dat",ios :: app);

while(rd1.read((char *) &d,sizeof(d)))
{
rd2.open("reftbl.dat",ios ::  in);
   while(rd2.read((char *) &t,sizeof(t)))
   {
     if(stricmp(d.mne,t.mne)==0)
     {
      if(stricmp(d.data,"")==0)
      {
  if(f.lcode==8010 ||f.lcode==8011 ||f.lcode==8012 ||f.lcode==8013 ||f.lcode==8014 ||
f.lcode==8015)
 {
     if(f.lcode==8010 && tno==1)
     {
      strcpy(f.loc,"800A");
     }
     else
      if(f.lcode==8011 && tno==1)
      {
      strcpy(f.loc,"800B");
      }
      else
       if(f.lcode==8012 && tno==1)
       {
       strcpy(f.loc,"800C");
       }
       else
       if(f.lcode==8013 && tno==1)
       {
       strcpy(f.loc,"800D");
       }
       else
       if(f.lcode==8014 && tno==1)
       {
```

```
        strcpy(f.loc,"800E");
        tno++;
        }
        else
        if(f.lcode==8015 && tno==1)
        {
        strcpy(f.loc,"800F");
        tno++;
        }
       wr1.write((char *) &f,sizeof(f));
       cout<<f.loc<<" "<<t.opcode;
       cout<<"\n";
    f.lcode=f.lcode+t.len;
 }
   else
   {
    if(tno>1)
    {
     f.lcode=8010;
    }
     wr1.write((char *) &f,sizeof(f));
    cout<<f.lcode<<" "<<t.opcode;
    cout<<"\n";
    f.lcode=f.lcode+t.len;
   }
    }
    else
    {
 if(f.lcode==8010 || f.lcode==8011 || f.lcode==8012 || f.lcode==8013 || f.lcode==8014
|| f.lcode==8015)
 {
    if(f.lcode==8010 && tno==1)
    {
     strcpy(f.loc,"800A");
    }
    else
     if(f.lcode==8011 && tno==1)
```

```
{
strcpy(f.loc,"800B");
}
else
if(f.lcode==8012 && tno==1)
{
strcpy(f.loc,"800C");
}
else
if(f.lcode==8013 && tno==1)
{
strcpy(f.loc,"800D");
}
else
if(f.lcode==8014 && tno==1)
{
strcpy(f.loc,"800E");
tno++;
}
else
if(f.lcode==8015 && tno==1)
{
strcpy(f.loc,"800F");
tno++;
}
wr1.write((char *) &f,sizeof(f));
cout<<f.loc<<" "<<t.opcode<<" "<<d.data;
cout<<"\n";
f.lcode=f.lcode+t.len;
}
else
{
if(tno>1)
{
f.lcode=8010;
```

```
	}
	 wr1.write((char *) &f,sizeof(f));
	 cout<<f.lcode<<" "<<t.opcode<<" "<<d.data;
	 cout<<"\n";
	 f.lcode=f.lcode+t.len;
	 }
	 }
	 }

	}
/*	 wr1.write((char *) &f,sizeof(f));*/
	rd2.close();
}
}

void compare2()
{
ifstream cd1;
ifstream cd2;
ofstream cr1;
outfile_data f;
refer_data d;
table_data t;
tno=1;
 cd1.open("forref.dat",ios :: in);
 if(cd1.fail())
 {
 cout<<"\n File Open Error";
 exit(1);
 }
/* if(rd2.fail())
 {
 cout<<"\n File Open Error";
 exit(1);
} */
```

```
cr1.close();
cr1.open("forout2.dat",ios :: app);

while(cd1.read((char *) &d,sizeof(d)))
{
cd2.open("reftbl.dat",ios ::  in);
    while(cd2.read((char *) &t,sizeof(t)))
    {
/*        if(stricmp(d.mne,t.mne)==0)
        {
          if(stricmp(t.data,"")==1)
          {*/
if((stricmp(d.lbel,d.lbel)==0) && (stricmp(d.mne,"JNC")==0) && (stricmp (t.mne,"OUT")
==0))
{
if(f.lcode==8010 || f.lcode==8011 || f.lcode==8012 || f.lcode==8013 || f.lcode==8014
|| f.lcode==8015)
 {
      if(f.lcode==8010 && tno==1)
      {
       strcpy(f.loc,"800A");
       }
       else
        if(f.lcode==8011 && tno==1)
        {
        strcpy(f.loc,"800B");
        tno++;
        }
        else
         if(f.lcode==8012 && tno==1)
         {
         strcpy(f.loc,"800C");
         tno++;
         }
         else
         if(f.lcode==8013 && tno==1)
         {
```

```
            strcpy(f.loc,"800D");
            tno++;
            }
            else
            if(f.lcode==8014 && tno==1)
            {
            strcpy(f.loc,"800E");
            tno++;
            }
            else
            if(f.lcode==8015 && tno==1)
            {
            strcpy(f.loc,"800F");
            tno++;
            }
            strcpy(f.lbel,d.lbel);
           cr1.write((char *) &f,sizeof(f));
           cout<<f.loc<<" "<<d.lbel;
           cout<<"\n";
        f.lcode=f.lcode+t.len;
        break;
    }
      else
      {
       if(tno>1)
       {
        f.lcode=8010;
        }
   /*         cout<<f.lcode<<" "<<t.opcode;
        cout<<"\n";*/
        f.lcode=f.lcode+t.len;
      }
        }
        else
        {
   if(f.lcode==8010 || f.lcode==8011 || f.lcode==8012 || f.lcode==8013 || f.lcode==8014
|| f.lcode==8015)
```

```
{
    if(f.lcode==8010 && tno==1)
    {
     strcpy(f.loc,"800A");
     }
     else
      if(f.lcode==8011 && tno==1)
      {
      strcpy(f.loc,"800B");
      tno++;
      }
       else
       if(f.lcode==8012 && tno==1)
       {
       strcpy(f.loc,"800C");
       tno++;
       }
       else
       if(f.lcode==8013 && tno==1)
       {
       strcpy(f.loc,"800D");
       tno++;
       }
       else
       if(f.lcode==8014 && tno==1)
       {
       strcpy(f.loc,"800E");
       tno++;
       }
       else
       if(f.lcode==8015 && tno==1)
       {
       strcpy(f.loc,"800F");
       tno++;
       }
/*    cout<<f.loc<<" "<<t.opcode<<" "<<d.data;
```

```
    cout<<"\n";*/

   f.lcode=f.lcode+t.len;
 }
  else
    {
   if(tno>1)
   {
   f.lcode=8010;
   }
/*      cout<<f.lcode<<" "<<t.opcode<<" "<<d.data;
    cout<<"\n";*/
    f.lcode=f.lcode+t.len;
    }
    }
/*      }*/

  }
/*    cr1.write((char *) &f,sizeof(f));*/
  cd2.close();

}
}
```

Symbol Input File

```
#include<fstream.h>
#include<conio.h>
#include<stdlib.h>
#include<stdio.h>
#include<ctype.h>

class simple_data
{
 private :
    char mne[20],data[20];
```

```
public :
        void entry();
        void display();
};

main()
{
clrscr();

simple_data s;

ofstream wr;
ifstream rd;

wr.open("simple_data.dat",ios :: app);

if(wr.fail())
{
cerr<<"File creation error";
exit(1);
}

char con;

do
{
s.entry();

wr.write((char *) &s,sizeof(s));

cout<<"\n Continue (y/n)";
con=getche();
}while(tolower(con)=='y');

wr.close();
```

```
rd.open("simple_data.dat",ios :: in);

if(rd.fail())
{
cerr<<"File Open Error";
exit(1);
}

while(rd.read((char *) &s,sizeof(s)))
{
s.display();
}
rd.close();


getch();
}

void simple_data :: entry()
{
clrscr();
cout<<"Enter The Mne-Code";
fflush(stdin);
gets(mne);
cout<<"Enter The Data";
fflush(stdin);
gets(data);
}

void simple_data :: display()
{
cout<<"\n";
cout<<"\n Mne-Code : "<<mne;
cout<<"\n Data       : "<<data;

}
```

Comparison For Symbol Table

```
#include<fstream.h>
#include<conio.h>
#include<stdlib.h>
#include<stdio.h>
#include<string.h>

class outfile_data
{
 private :
        long int lcode;
        char mne[20];
        char loc[15];

 public :
        outfile_data();
        friend void compare();
        void display();
};


class simple_data
{
 private :
        char mne[20],data[20];

 public :
        friend void compare();
};


class table_data
{
 private :
        char mne[20],data[20],opcode[20];
        int len;
```

```
 public :
      friend void compare();
};

int tno;

main()
{
clrscr();
void compare();


ofstream wr1;

ifstream rd1;
ifstream rd2;
ifstream rd3;


if(wr1.fail())
{
cerr<<"File creation error";
exit(1);
}

char con;

compare();

getch();
}

outfile_data :: outfile_data()
{
lcode=8000;
```

```
}

void compare()
{
ifstream rd1;
ifstream rd2;
ofstream wr1;
outfile_data f;
simple_data  d;
table_data   t;


 rd1.open("simple_data.dat",ios :: in);
 if(rd1.fail())
 {
 cout<<"\n File Open Error";
 exit(1);
 }
 if(rd2.fail())
 {
 cout<<"\n File Open Error";
 exit(1);
}

wr1.open("outsimple.dat",ios :: app);

while(rd1.read((char *) &d,sizeof(d)))
{
rd2.open("table.dat",ios ::  in);
    while(rd2.read((char *) &t,sizeof(t)))
    {
      if(stricmp(d.mne,t.mne)==0)
      {
       if(stricmp(d.data,"")==0)
       {
if(f.lcode==8010 || f.lcode==8011 || f.lcode==8012 || f.lcode==8013 || f.lcode==8014
```

```
|| f.lcode==8015)
{
    if(f.lcode==8010 && tno==1)
    {
     strcpy(f.loc,"800A");
    }
    else
     if(f.lcode==8011 && tno==1)
     {
     strcpy(f.loc,"800B");
     }
     else
      if(f.lcode==8012 && tno==1)
      {
      strcpy(f.loc,"800C");
      }
      else
      if(f.lcode==8013 && tno==1)
      {
      strcpy(f.loc,"800D");
      }
      else
      if(f.lcode==8014 && tno==1)
      {
      strcpy(f.loc,"800E");
      }
      else
      if(f.lcode==8015 && tno==1)
      {
      strcpy(f.loc,"800F");
      tno++;
      }

     cout<<f.loc<<" "<<t.opcode;
   f.lcode=f.lcode+t.len;
}
```

```
else
{
  if(tno>1)
  {
   f.lcode=8010;
  }
   cout<<f.lcode<<" "<<t.opcode;
   cout<<"\n";
   f.lcode=f.lcode+t.len;
}
   }
   else
   {
    if(f.lcode==8010 || f.lcode==8011 || f.lcode==8012 || f.lcode==8013 || f.lcode==8014
|| f.lcode==8015)
    {
      if(f.lcode==8010 && tno==1)
      {
       strcpy(f.loc, "800A");
      }
       else
        if(f.lcode==8011 && tno==1)
        {
        strcpy(f.loc, "800B");
        }
         else
         if(f.lcode==8012 && tno==1)
         {
         strcpy(f.loc, "800C");
         }
         else
         if(f.lcode==8013 && tno==1)
         {
         strcpy(f.loc,"800D");
         }
         else
         if(f.lcode==8014 && tno==1)
```

```
{
strcpy(f.loc,"800E");
}
else
if(f.lcode==8015 && tno==1)
{
strcpy(f.loc,"800F");
tno++;
}
cout<<f.loc<<" "<<t.opcode;
f.lcode=f.lcode+t.len;
}
else
{
if(tno>1)
{
f.lcode=8010;
}
cout<<f.lcode<<" "<<t.opcode<<" "<<d.data;
cout<<"\n";
f.lcode=f.lcode+t.len;
}
}
}

}
wr1.write((char *) &f,sizeof(f));
rd2.close();
}
}
```

Symbol Table File

```
#include<fstream.h>
#include<conio.h>
#include<stdlib.h>
#include<stdio.h>

class table_data
```

```
{
 private :
      char mne[20],data[20],opcode[20];
      int len;

 public :
       void entry();
       void display();
};

main()
{
clrscr();

table_data p;

ofstream wr;
ifstream rd;

wr.open("table.dat",ios :: app);

if(wr.fail())
{
cerr<<"File creation error";
exit(1);
}

char con;

do
{
p.entry();

wr.write((char *) &p,sizeof(p));

cout<<"\n Continue (y/n)";
```

```
con=getche();
}while(con=='y');

wr.close();

rd.open("table.dat",ios :: in);

if(rd.fail())
{
cerr<<"File Open Error";
exit(1);
}

while(rd.read((char *) &p,sizeof(p)))
{
p.display();
}
rd.close();


getch();
}

void table_data :: entry()
{
clrscr();
cout<<"Enter The Mne-Code";
fflush(stdin);
gets(mne);
cout<<"Enter The Data";
fflush(stdin);
gets(data);
cout<<"Enter The Op_code";
fflush(stdin);
gets(opcode);
cout<<"Enter Length";
```

```
cin>>len;
}

void table_data :: display()
{
cout<<"\n";
cout<<"\n Mne-Code : "<<mne;
cout<<"\n Data      : "<<data;
cout<<"\n Op_code   : "<<opcode;
cout<<"\n Length    : "<<len;
}
```

Pass2

```
#include<fstream.h>
#include<conio.h>
#include<stdlib.h>
#include<stdio.h>
#include<string.h>

class outfile_data
{
 private :
        char mne[20];
        char data[15];
        char lbel[15];

 public :
       /*outfile_data();*/
       friend void compare1();
       friend void compare2();
       void display();
};


class refer_data
{
 private :
```

```
        char mne[20],data[20],lbel[15];

    public :
        friend void compare1();
        friend void compare2();
    };


    class table_data
    {
     private :
        char mne[20],data[20];
        int len;

     public :
        friend void compare1();
        friend void compare2();
    };

    int tno=1;

    struct time
    {
        char ti_min;
        char ti_hour;
        char ti_hund;
        char ti_sec;
    }t;

    main()
    {
    clrscr();
    void compare1();
    void compare2();
```

```
ofstream wr1;

ifstream rd1;
ifstream rd2;
ifstream rd3;

if(wr1.fail())
{
cerr<<"File creation error";
exit(1);
}

char con;

cout<<"\n Pass2 Datas";
cout<<"\n ===========";
cout<<"\n";
compare1();

/*compare2();*/

getch();
}
/*outfile_data :: outfile_data()
{
lcode=8000;
spl='-';
} */

void compare1()
{
ifstream rd1;
ifstream rd2;
ofstream wr1;
outfile_data f;
refer_data d;
```

```
table_data t;

wr1.close();
 rd1.open("tryout.dat",ios :: in);
 if(rd1.fail())
 {
 cout<<"\n File Open Error";
 exit(1);
 }
/* if(rd2.fail())
 {
 cout<<"\n File Open Error";
 exit(1);
 } */

wr1.open("pass2.dat",ios :: app);

while(rd1.read((char *) &d,sizeof(d)))
{
rd2.open("tryout2.dat",ios ::  in);
rd2.read((char *) &t,sizeof(t));
/*     while(rd2.read((char *) &t,sizeof(t)))
      {*/
       if(stricmp(t.data,"LOOP")==0)
       {
      if(stricmp(d.lbel,"-")==0)
      {
         gettime(&t);
         cout<<d.mne<<" "<<d.data<<"  "<<t.mne;
         cout<<"\n\n Eecutuin Time Period : <<ti_sec <<"Seconds";
         strcpy(f.mne,d.mne);
         strcpy(f.data,d.data);
         strcpy(f.lbel,d.lbel);

         wr1.write((char *) &f,sizeof(f));
         cout<<"\n";
```

```
/*      f.lcode=f.lcode+t.len;*/

        }
        else
        {
        cout<<d.mne<<" "<<d.data<<"   "<<d.lbel;
         strcpy(f.mne,d.mne);
         strcpy(f.data,d.data);
         strcpy(f.lbel,d.lbel);
         wr1.write((char *) &f,sizeof(f));
         cout<<"\n";
       }
       }
       }
  }
}
```

BIBLIOGRAPHY

1. Leland L. Beck, System Software: An Introduction to Systems Programming, Pearson Education Asia, 2001.
2. James L. Antonakos, An Introduction to the Intel Family of Microprocessors, Pearson Education Asia, 1999.
3. Alfred V. Aho, Ravi Sethi, Jeffrey D. Ullman, Compilers, Principles, Techniques and Tools, International Student Edition, 1999.
4. Steven. S. Muchnik, Advanced Compiler Design and Implementation, Harcourt Asia, 2000.
5. A.V. Aho, Ravi Sethi and J.D.Ullman, "Compilers Principles, Techniques and Tools. Addison Wesley, 1998.
6. High-level code improving transformations for Java programming language—project work done by M. Joseph, K. Aishwarya (2001).
7. Inter procedural analysis and optimizations—project work done by M. Joseph, J. Niraimathi (2002).
8. Construction of 8085 Assembler—project work done by M. Joseph, R. Bargavi (2003).
9. An analytical study of data structures for symbol table in assemblers—project work done by M. Joseph, B. Santhi (2003).
10. Steven S. Muchnik, Advanced Compiler design and Implementation, Harcourt Asia publications, 2000.

INDEX

8085 Microprocessor 5

A

Absolute loader 130, 131, 139, 140
Accumulator 7, 9, 10, 11, 14, 15, 17
Address bus 5, 7, 12, 20
Address descriptor 91
Addressing modes 5, 10, 14, 15, 20, 26, 27
Ambiguous grammar 64, 90
Argument List (AL) 123
Arithmetic and logic instructions 9, 14
Arithmetic and Logic Unit (ALU) 13
Arithmetic Logic Instructions 17
Assembler directives 98, 100, 102, 103, 104, 110, 112, 113
Assemblers 1, 2, 96, 98, 100, 101, 102, 103, 104, 105, 109, 111, 112, 113
Assembly language program 5, 8, 11, 12, 18, 19, 26, 27
Assume 99, 100, 104
Attributes 57, 76, 78, 79, 85
Augmented grammar 90, 71

B

Based indexed addressing mode 15, 16
Basic blocks 95
Batch Monitor 30
Batch processing 29, 30, 52
Bit Manipulation Instructions 16, 17, 23
Bootstrap loader 131, 139, 140
Botom up Parsers 65
Break Point Method 147, 148, 149
Bus Interface Unit (BIU) 12
Buses 5, 20

C

Closed subroutines 116, 117, 127
Closure function 71, 73
Code generation 56, 76, 88, 91, 95
Code generator 53, 56, 57, 80, 88, 91
Code Motion or Loop Invariant Computation 85
Code optimization 55, 85, 86
Code optimization 86
Code optimizer 53, 56, 57, 90
Common sub-expression elimination 84, 88
Compaction 41, 42, 52
Compile and Go Loaders 130
Compiler 53, 54, 55, 56, 57, 78, 81, 82, 84, 85, 86, 91, 94
Compilers 1, 2

Computation of First 67
Computation of Follow 68
Conditional Macros 123
Constant Folding 86
Constant Propagation 86, 87
Context Free Grammars (CFG) 62
context switching 31, 32, 33
Control Bus 5, 7
Control instructions 9, 13, 16, 18, 25
Control Unit and Instruction Decoder 13

D

Data bus 5, 7, 12, 20, 27
Data Formats 8
Data Store 143, 144
Data structures for two pass assembler construction 103
Data transfer instructions 9, 16, 17, 21
Dead Code Elimination 88
Debuggers 146, 147, 149
DEBUGGERS 146
Demand paging 47, 48, 49
Derivations and Reductions 63
Design of two Pass Assemblers 102
Deterministic Finite Automata (DFA) 59, 60
Direct addressing mode 11, 15
Direct addressing 10, 11, 15
Dynamic linking 138, 139, 140

E

Editors and Debuggers 3
Editors 145, 146, 149
Error handler 56, 82
Errors 54, 56, 57, 67, 71, 76, 84, 85, 91
Execution Unit (EU) 12
Execution unit 12, 13, 20
Execution unit 20, 21
External Fragmentation 41, 43, 47, 52
External Symbol Table 112
External Symbols 112

F

Finite automata 59, 60, 93
First Come First Served Scheduling (FCFS) 33
First In First Out (FIFO) algorithm 49
Flag register 7, 13, 22
Flow Graphs 91
Forward reference 100, 101, 102, 109, 112, 113, 114

G

General purpose registers 13, 14
Getreg 93
Goto function 71, 73

H

Hash Tables 106

I

Immediate Addressing Mode 15
Immediate Addressing 10, 15, 26
Indirect Addressing Mode 15, 16
Indirect Addressing 10, 11, 15, 16
Indirect Triples 83, 84
Induction variable elimination 89, 90
Inherited attributes 77, 78, 79
Inherited Translation 76, 79, 80
Instruction costs 91
Instruction format 5, 9, 27
Instruction Pointer (IP) 13
Instruction Queue (IQ) 12
Instruction set of 8086 16
Instruction set 5, 8, 11, 12, 16, 18, 19, 21, 26, 27
Instruction Types 21

Intel 80286 19, 27
Intel 80386 20, 27
Intel 80486 20, 27
Intermediate code generation 56, 76
Internal Fragmentation 42, 43, 46, 52
Interpretation 141, 142, 143, 144, 145, 149
Interpreter 54, 141, 142, 143, 149
interpreters 142, 144, 149

J

Java 141, 142, 144, 145, 149

K

Kleene Closure 57

L

Labels in Macros 126
Left Factoring 68
Left Recursion 67, 68
Lexical Analyser 55
Linear List 106
Linkage Editors 137
Linkers 1, 2
Linking Loaders 130, 132, 134, 135
Literal Table (LT) 102, 104, 105, 110
Loaders 1, 2, 129, 130, 131, 132, 134, 135, 136, 138, 140
Location Counter 99, 102, 103, 104, 105, 107, 108, 109, 110, 112, 113
Logical Address and Physical Address 37
Loop Optimizations 88, 89
Loops 86, 89
LR PARSERS 70
LR parsers 72, 95

M

Macro Definition Table (MDT) 123
Macro Name Table (MNT) 122, 123
Macro Operators 125
Macro Processor Design 122, 123
Macro Processors 115, 118, 122, 123, 127
Macros and Macro Processors 3, 4
Macros with Parameters 121
macros 115, 116, 117, 118, 119, 120, 121, 122, 124, 125, 126, 127, 128
Memory Allocation Schemes 36, 41, 52
Memory Management 28, 31, 35, 36, 43, 51, 52
Microprograms 143
Mnemonics Table (MT) 103, 104, 109, 110
Multi Pass Assemblers 101, 102
Multiple partition allocation 38, 46
Multiprogramming 30, 31, 32, 33, 35

N

Next-Use Information 92
Non-Deterministic Finite Automata (NFA) 59
Non-Recursive Predictive Parser 68
Non-terminals 65, 68, 70, 71, 75, 81

O

Object module 129, 130, 131, 132, 133, 134, 135, 136, 137, 138, 139
Opcode 97, 100, 103, 104, 108, 110, 111, 113
Open Subroutines 116, 117
Operating system techniques 29, 35, 51, 52
Operating System 1, 3, 28, 29, 30, 31, 32, 33, 34, 35, 36, 37, 38, 41, 43, 47, 49, 51, 52

P

Page replacement in FIFO algorithm 51
Page replacement 49, 51, 52
Paging 43, 44, 45, 46, 47, 48, 49, 51, 52
Parse trees 64, 65, 81
Parsers 66, 67, 71, 72, 95
Parsers 67
Parsing Algorithm 69, 70

Parsing table 68, 69, 70, 72, 75, 76
Particular free space of memory can be called as a hole 38
Phases and Passes 56
Pointers and index registers 14
Positive Closure 57
Postfix 56, 95
Preprocessor 3, 4
Preprocessors 115, 127
Priority Scheduling 34
Process 28, 29, 30, 31, 32, 33, 34, 35, 37, 38, 39, 40, 41, 42, 43, 46, 47, 49, 51, 52
Production Rule 64
Program Counter (PC) 6, 8
Pseudo Instruction Table (PIT) 104, 109, 110

Q

Quadruples 79
Quadruples, Triples and Indirect Triples 79

R

Reduction in strength 89, 90
Register Addressing Mode 15
Register addressing 10, 11, 15
Register descriptor 92, 93, 94
Register relative addressing mode 15
Registers 5, 7, 11, 12, 13, 14, 15, 16, 19, 20, 21, 22, 27
Regular Expressions (RE) 58
Regular Expressions 58, 59, 60
Relative based indexed addressing mode 15
Relocating loaders 130, 132, 138
Relocation 111, 113, 132, 133, 134, 135, 136, 137, 138, 139
RISC and CISC Machines 141, 142

S

Scheduling 32, 33, 34, 51, 52
Segment Registers 12
Segment registers 12, 13, 20
Segmentation 46, 47
Shortest Job First Scheduling (SJF) 34
Single Partition Allocation 36, 37
Single Pass Assemblers 101
Single Step Control 147, 148, 149
SLR Parser 72
Stack Pointer (SP) 7, 8, 14
Start symbol 62, 70, 73
String instructions 16, 18, 23
Subroutines 115, 116, 117, 121, 127
Swapping 35, 42, 47, 48, 52
Symbol Table (ST) 103, 104
Symbol table management 102, 103, 105
Symbol table 56, 84, 85, 93, 143, 144
Syntax Analyser 55
Syntax Directed Translation (SDT) 56, 75
Syntax Trees 77
Synthesized attributes 77, 78
Synthesized translation 75, 76
System software 1, 2, 3, 4

T

Terminals 64, 65, 68, 69, 70, 75, 81, 95
Threads 32, 52
Three address codes 56, 93, 94
Three Address Codes 81
Time sharing 31, 33, 37
Tokens 57, 58, 59, 64, 65, 67, 95
Top-Down Parsers 65
Transition table 60, 95
Translation 53, 54, 55, 56, 78, 79, 80, 94
Triples 80
Two pass assemblers 101, 102, 109

V

Variable Propagation or Copy Propagation 87
virtual memory 47, 48, 51

FIREWALL MEDIA

(An imprint of Laxmi Publications Pvt. Ltd.)

Computer Books *for School, BCA, MCA, IGNOU, DOEACC and Engineering Students and Professionals*

ISBN	TITLE	AUTHOR	PRICE	PAGES
	.NET			
8170087155	**Building Business Intelligence Applications with .Net**	Robert Ericsson	Rs. 295.00	404
8170083567	**Learning VB.Net Through Applications**	Clayton Crooks	Rs. 295.00	450
8131800865	**Magic of C# with .Net Frame Work**	Shibi Panikkar, Kumar Sanjeev	Rs. 495.00	950
8170082471	**Magic of ASP.Net with C#**	Shibi Panikkar, Kumar Sanjeev	Rs. 395.00	828
8170089662	**ASP.Net Interview Questions and Answers**	J. Rajaram	Rs. 95.00	175
	A TO Z SERIES			
8170083214	**Access 2002 from A to Z**	Julia Kelly, Stephen L. Nelson	Rs. 75.00	185
8170083222	**Excel 2002 from A to Z**	Stephen L. Nelson	Rs. 75.00	193
8170083230	**Front Page 2002 from A to Z**	Heather Williamson	Rs. 85.00	219
8170083249	**Outlook 2002 from A to Z**	Stephen L. Nelson	Rs. 75.00	202
8170083257	**Page Maker 7 from A to Z**	Marc Campbell	Rs. 75.00	202
8170083265	**PowerPoint 2002 from A to Z**	Stephen L. Nelson	Rs. 75.00	202
8170083273	**Windows XP from A to Z**	Pat Coleman	Rs. 95.00	249
8170083281	**Word 2002 from A to Z**	Stephen L. Nelson	Rs. 75.00	199
817008329X	**XML from A to Z**	Heather Williamson	Rs. 75.00	200
8170083303	**Dreamweaver 4 from A to Z**	Heather Williamson	Rs. 85.00	215
	BEGINNERS & GENERAL INTEREST			
817008248X	**Shortcuts to Success in Computing**	Dheeraj Mehrotra	Rs. 55.00	110
8170083311	**Pictorial Computer Dictionary**	Dheeraj Mehrotra	Rs. 45.00	156
8170083486	**Pocket Net Browser**	Dheeraj Mehrotra	Rs. 95.00	302
8170084261	**1000 IT Quizzes**	Dheeraj Mehrotra	Rs. 75.00	120
8131800679	**Information Technology Bible**	Remesh Bangia	Rs. 295.00	567
8131800377	**Fundamentals of Information Technology Including MS Office**	Dinesh Maidasani, Jai Narayan Yadav	Rs. 175.00	356
813180089X	**Fundamentals of Information Technology Including MS Office (Hindi Medium)**	Dinesh Maidasani, Jai Narayan Yadav	Rs. 175.00	425
8170089719	**Foundations of Computer Science**	Ashok Arora	Rs. 250.00	386

Please write for a free color Firewall Media Catalog for details on the above books.

ISBN	TITLE	AUTHOR	PRICE	PAGES
	CALL CENTERS			
8170082196	**Call Centers Made Easy**	Stephen Medcroft	Rs. 195.00	310
	CISCO			
8170087481	**Enabling IP Routing with Cisco Routers**	R. Das, K. Chakrabarty	Rs. 295.00	486
817008749X	**Designing Networks with Cisco**	H. Pasricha, D. Jagu	Rs. 195.00	316
8170087503	**Cisco IP Routing Protocols: Troubleshooting Techniques**	V. Anand, K. Chakrabarty	Rs. 295.00	409
	DATABASES			
8170089530	**DBMS—Complete Practical Approach**	Sharad Maheshwari, Ruchin Jain	Rs. 350.00	656
8170082404	**Learn to Program Visual Basic-Examples**	John Smiley	Rs. 295.00	482
8170082412	**Learn to Program Visual Basic-Databases**	John Smiley	Rs. 325.00	653
8170082420	**Learn to Program Visual Basic-Objects**	John Smiley	Rs. 325.00	670
817008475X	**IT Resources-Access 2002 VBA Programming Access**	Michele Amelot	Rs. 195.00	424
8170084512	**The Power of Oracle 9i**	Rajiv Parida, Vinod Sharma	Rs. 475.00	1035
8170088518	**Principles and Implementation of Data Warehousing**	Rajiv A. Parida	Rs. 295.00	487
817008864X	**DBA Study Guide OCP Prep Guide**	Nazar Abdul	Rs. 295.00	474
8170088658	**Oracle 11i—The Complete Reference**	Rashmi Anandi	Rs. 495.00	975
8131800067	**Toxonomy of Database Management System**	Aditya Kumar Gupta	Rs. 75.00	146
8131800385	**Introduction to SQL and PL/SQL**	Sharad Maheshwari, Ruchin Jain	Rs. 200.00	389
	DOEACC 'O' LEVEL			
8170088089	**DOEACC 'O' Level Model Test Papers**	Ramesh Bangia	Rs. 175.00	296
8170089115	**DOEACC 'O' & 'A' Level Programming & Problem Solving Through 'C' Language (Model Test Paper with Solutions)**	Mukesh Sharma	Rs. 95.00	213
8170089069	**DOEACC 'O' & 'A' Level Business Systems (Model Test Paper with Solutions)**	Mukesh Sharma	Rs. 100.00	252
8170085640	**Programming and Problem Solving Through "C" Language**	Harsha Priya, R. Ranjeet	Rs. 95.00	306

ISBN	TITLE	AUTHOR	PRICE	PAGES
8170084474	**IT Tools and Applications**	Ramesh Bangia	Rs. 145.00	370
8170085594	**Business Systems**	Ramesh Bangia	Rs. 175.00	452
8170089514	**Internet & Web Design**	Ramesh Bangia	Rs. 150.00	300

ELECTRONIC COMMERCE

ISBN	TITLE	AUTHOR	PRICE	PAGES
8170085497	**Electronic Commerce**	Pete Loshin, John Vacca	Rs. 295.00	472
817008119X	**E-Commerce**	Mamta Bhusry	Rs. 95.00	215
8170083524	**Marketing in the Cyber Age**	Kurt Rohner	Rs. 295.00	223

HARDWARE/EMBEDDED SYSTEMS

ISBN	TITLE	AUTHOR	PRICE	PAGES
8170087473	**Essential Electronics for PC Technicians**	John W. Farber	Rs. 295.00	546
8170086264	**Grid Computing: A Practical Guide to Technology and Applications**	Ahmar Abbas	Rs. 295.00	408
8170088186	**CD Cracking Uncovered Protection Against Unsanctioned CD Copy**	Kris Kaspersky	Rs. 295.00	422
8170083435	**Practical Linux Programming: Device Drivers, Embedded Systems and the Internet**	Ashfaq A. Khan	Rs. 295.00	420
8170083575	**TCP/IP Application Layer Protocols for Embedded Systems**	M. Tim Jones	Rs. 295.00	460
8131800520	**PC Repair and Maintenance : A Practical Guide**	Joel Rosenthal, Kevin irwin	Rs. 195.00	362
8131800768	**The A+ Certification and PC Repair Handbook**	Christopher A Crayton, Joel Z. Rosenthal	Rs. 495.00	888

INTERNET & WEB TECHNOLOGY

ISBN	TITLE	AUTHOR	PRICE	PAGES
8170083206	**The Internet Handbook for Writers, Students and Teachers**	Mary McGuire, Linda Stilborne	Rs. 195.00	276
8170084776	**Way in-Internet Getting Started**	Elizabeth Bramire	Rs. 95.00	165
8170088976	**Web Technology**	Ramesh Bangia	Rs. 250.00	560
8170087163	**Web Design with Macromedia Studio MX 2004**	Eric Hunley	Rs. 295.00	558
8170083400	**Professional Web Design (Techniques and Templates)**	Clint Eccher	Rs. 295.00	425
8170088046	**HTML, XHTML, CSS and XML**	Teodoru Gugoiu	Rs. 195.00	355
8170083583	**FrontPage 2000 for Visual Learners**	Chris Charuhas	Rs. 95.00	200
8170083591	**HTML & Java Script for Visual Learners**	Chris Charuhas	Rs. 95.00	200

ISBN	TITLE	AUTHOR	PRICE	PAGES
8170083605	**The Visual Learners Guide to Managing Web Projects**	Chris Charuhas	Rs. 95.00	130
8170083613	**Dreamweaver 4 for Visual Learners**	Chris Charuhas	Rs. 95.00	200
8170084768	**IT Resource-Implementing XML: Managing and Formatting Data**	Johhny Brochard	Rs. 125.00	279
8170089476	**Design Your Web World**	Sunil Jalota	Rs. 75.00	146

KEEPING AHEAD SERIES

ISBN	TITLE	AUTHOR	PRICE	PAGES
8170084652	**Keeping Ahead-Exchange 2000 Server**	Philippe Levesque	Rs. 145.00	285
8170084660	**Keeping Ahead-Windows 2000 Professional**	Jose Dardoigne	Rs. 175.00	388
8170084679	**Keeping Ahead-Windows 2000 Server**	Philippe Mathon	Rs. 175.00	360
8170084687	**Keeping Ahead-Linux Administration Kernel Version 2.0 to 2.2**	Bruno Guèrin	Rs. 125.00	240
8170084695	**Keeping Ahead-Using Linux Kernel Version 2.0 to 2.2**	Bruno Guèrin	Rs. 125.00	258
8170084709	**Keeping Ahead-Java 2**	Benjamin Aumaille	Rs. 145.00	284
8170084717	**Keeping Ahead-SQL Server 7**	Joelle Mosset	Rs. 145.00	329
8170084725	**Keeping Ahead-JavaScript and VBScript**	Benjamin Aumaille	Rs. 145.00	313
8170084733	**Keeping Ahead-C++ Programming Language**	Bruno Dubois	Rs. 125.00	234
8170084741	**Keeping Ahead-TCP/IP in the NT Environment**	Bruno Ferec	Rs. 125.00	230

MCSE

ISBN	TITLE	AUTHOR	PRICE	PAGES
817008489X	**MCSE-Administering SQL Server 7.0**	Jerome Gabillaud	Rs. 295.00	580
8170084903	**MCSE-Networking Essentials**	Jose Dordoigne	Rs. 245.00	453
8170084911	**MCSE-Windows 2000 Professional**	Jose Dordoigne	Rs. 325.00	665
817008492X	**MCSE-Windows 2000 Server**	Phillippe Mathon	Rs. 345.00	712

MULTIMEDIA AND ANIMATION

ISBN	TITLE	AUTHOR	PRICE	PAGES
8170088208	**3DS Max 6 Animation with Character Studio 4 and Plug-Ins**	Boris Kulagin, Dmitry Morozov	Rs. 175.00	216

Please write for a free color Firewall Media Catalog for details on the above books.

ISBN	TITLE	AUTHOR	PRICE	PAGES
8170088216	**Adobe Audition: Soundtracks for Digital Video**	Roman Petelin, Yury Petelin	Rs. 195.00	278
8170086205	**Building A Digital Human**	Ken Brilliant	Rs. 295.00	380
8170086213	**Making Digital Videos**	Ben Long	Rs. 295.00	284
8170087171	**Illustrating with Macromedia Flash ™ MX2004**	Robert Firbaugh	Rs. 245.00	366
8170082439	**Multimedia Basics-Technology (Vol. I)**	Andreas Holzinger	Rs. 195.00	312
8170082447	**Multimedia Basics-Learning (Vol. II)**	Andreas Holzinger	Rs. 195.00	326
8170082455	**Multimedia Basics-Design (Vol. III)**	Andreas Holzinger	Rs. 195.00	280
8170083532	**Maya Feature Creature Creations**	Todd Palamar	Rs. 295.00	376
8170083540	**Sound Forge Power**	Scott R. Garrigus	Rs. 195.00	344
8131800288	**Multimedia and Web Technology**	Ramesh Bangia	Rs. 395.00	878
813180044X	**Photoshop CS**	Shruti Lal	Rs. 195.00	434

NETWORKING

ISBN	TITLE	AUTHOR	PRICE	PAGES
817008721X	**Networking Essentials**	Jose Dordoigne	Rs. 195.00	453
8170089328	**TCP/IP Distributed System**	Vivek Acharya	Rs. 250.00	474
8170087023	**Computer Networks**	Ajit Kumar Singh	Rs. 95.00	181
8131800148	**The Real—world Network Troubleshooting Manual**	Alan Sugano	Rs. 295.00	396
817008203X	**Telecom & Networking Glossary**	Robert Mastin	Rs. 300.00	250
8170082048	**Data Networking Made Easy**	Karen Patten	Rs. 360.00	350
8170082056	**Digital Convergence**	Andy Covell	Rs. 300.00	234

OFFICE AUTOMATION

ISBN	TITLE	AUTHOR	PRICE	PAGES
8170089891	**Desk Top Publishing**	Dinesh Maidasani	Rs. 150.00	311
8170087805	**Learning Computer Fundamentals, MS Office and Internet & Web Technology**	Dinesh Maidasani	Rs. 95.00	301
8170087686	**MS-Word 2000 Thumb-Rules and Details**	Snigdha Banerjee	Rs. 175.00	390
8170089239	**Computer Accounting with Tally 7.2**	Firewall Media	Rs. 195.00	330

ON YOUR SIDE SERIES

ISBN	TITLE	AUTHOR	PRICE	PAGES
8170084830	**On your Side-Powerpoint 2002**	Andrew Blackburn	Rs. 145.00	282
8170084849	**On your Side-Excel 2002**	Adrienne Tommy	Rs. 125.00	275

ISBN	TITLE	AUTHOR	PRICE	PAGES
8170084857	**On your Side-Word 2002**	Adrienne Tommy	Rs. 125.00	289
8170084865	**On your Side-Access 2002**	Adrienne Tommy	Rs. 125.00	303
8170084873	**On your Side-Frontpage 2002**	Andrew Blackburn	Rs. 95.00	245
8170084881	**On your Side-Windows XP**	Adrienne Tommy	Rs. 125.00	310

OPERATING SYSTEMS

ISBN	TITLE	AUTHOR	PRICE	PAGES
8170087236	**Linux—A Practical Approach**	B. Mohamed Ibrahim	Rs. 95.00	187
8170088623	**Red Hat Linux Study Guide**	Vijay Shekhar	Rs. 350.00	635
8170088631	**Red Hat Linux-The Complete Bible**	Vijay Shekhar	Rs. 545.00	1176
8170089581	**Unix and Shell Programming**	Archana Verma	Rs. 80.00	137
8170089131	**Operating System Concepts**	P.S. Gill	Rs. 95.00	181
8170083427	**The MS-Windows XP Professional Handbook**	Louis Columbus	Rs. 295.00	330
8170084784	**Way in-Windows XP Home Edition**	Andrew Blackburn	Rs. 95.00	183
8170086221	**Cyber Rookies—Operating System Fundamentals**	D. Irtegov	Rs. 295.00	498

PROGRAMMING

ISBN	TITLE	AUTHOR	PRICE	PAGES
8170087791	**The Art of Programming Through Flowcharts & Algorithms**	Anil Bikas Chaudhuri	Rs. 95.00	160
8170086248	**Preventative Programming Techniques: Avoid and Correct Common Mistakes**	Brian Hawkins	Rs. 295.00	322
8170083443	**Learning Computer Programming : It's not about Languages**	Mary Farrell	Rs. 295.00	375
8170086256	**Object-Oriented Programming: From Problem Solving to Java**	José M. Garrido	Rs. 295.00	360
817008931X	**Object-Oriented Programming-Concept and Implementation**	A. Rajesh	Rs. 95.00	182
8170089107	**Java: J2SE-5 A Practical Approach**	B. Mohammad Ibrahim	Rs. 175.00	332
8170089409	**Advance Java**	Gajendra Gupta	Rs. 175.00	305
8170088038	**Assembly Language Programming for Intel Processors Family**	Vasile Lungu	Rs. 295.00	577
8170088178	**The Assembly Programming Master Book**	Vlad Pirogov	Rs. 395.00	726
813180075X	**Java Messaging**	Eric Bruno	Rs. 295.00	480

Please write for a free color Firewall Media Catalog for details on the above books.

ISBN	TITLE	AUTHOR	PRICE	PAGES
	PROGRAMMING - C#, C, C++			
8170083702	**The Power of C#**	Rajiv Parida	Rs. 295.00	576
8170085632	**Mastering Graphics Programming in 'C'**	Sudhir Dawra	Rs. 145.00	286
8170088879	**Programming in C and Numerical Analysis**	J.B. Dixit	Rs. 350.00	355
8170087074	**Mastering C Programs**	J.B. Dixit	Rs. 195.00	434
8170081262	**Programming in C**	J.B. Dixit	Rs. 295.00	506
8170087619	**Unix and C Programming**	Ashok Arora, Shefali Bansal	Rs. 295.00	606
817008878X	**C Interview Questions and Answers**	J. Rajaram	Rs. 75.00	139
8170089034	**Pragmatic C**	R.K. Jangda	Rs. 150.00	258
8170086140	**Data Structure for 'C' Programming**	Ajay Kumar	Rs. 145.00	290
8170081270	**Programming in C++**	J.B. Dixit	Rs. 260.00	602
8170088194	**Hackish C++ Pranks & Tricks**	Michael Flenov	Rs. 245.00	326
8170082889	**Basics of C++ Programming**	Nishant Kundalia	Rs. 95.00	168
8170083648	**Mastering C++ Programs**	J.B. Dixit	Rs. 295.00	598
817008623X	**Cyber Rookies—C++ Programming Fundamentals**	Chuck Easttom	Rs. 295.00	417
8131800202	**Data Structure using C++**	N. Jayalakshmi	Rs. 65.00	126
8170089123	**C++ Made Easy**	T.D. Malhotra	Rs. 250.00	449
8131800393	**C++ & Introduction to C#**	T.D. Malhotra, Rajeev A. Parida, A. Rajesh	Rs. 200.00	440
8131800350	**OOPS with C++**	M. Jaya Prasad	Rs. 150.00	317
	SECURITY			
8170083419	**Computer Forensics : Computer Crime Scene Investigation**	John Vacca	Rs. 445.00	731
8131800156	**Computer Evidence (Collection and Preservation)**	Christopher L.T. Brown	Rs. 295.00	394
8170083494	**Firewall Architecture for the Enterprise**	Norbert Pohlmann, Tim Crothers	Rs. 295.00	480
8170086272	**Net Spies**	Andrew Gauntlett	Rs. 195.00	210
3826607546	**Firewall Systems**	Norbert Pohlmann	Rs. 1630.00	544
8131800504	**Homeland Security Techniques and Technologies**	Jesus Mena	Rs. 295.00	346

Please write for a free color Firewall Media Catalog for details on the above books.

ISBN	TITLE	AUTHOR	PRICE	PAGES
	ENGINEERING AND TECHNOLOGY			
817008718X	**Human Aspects of Software Engineering**	James E. Tomayko, Orit Hazzan	Rs. 195.00	338
8131800032	**Management Information Systems**	Avdhesh Gupta, Anurag Malik	Rs. 195.00	400
8170087953	**Human Computer Interaction**	Rajendra Ranjan Kumar	Rs. 95.00	210
8170088097	**Structured System Analysis and Design**	Preeti Gupta	Rs. 125.00	192
817008802X	**Autocad 2005 for Engineers**	Ionel Simion	Rs. 175.00	271
8170088054	**Digital Signal Processing Fundamentals**	Ashfaq A. Khan	Rs. 295.00	391
8131800164	**Digital Communication System Using System VUE**	Dennis Silage	Rs. 295.00	365
8170089719	**Foundations of Computer Science**	Ashok Arora	Rs. 250.00	386
817008363X	**Practical Project Management**	Ivan Bayross	Rs. 195.00	342
8131800806	**Digital Signal Processing using MATLAB and Wavelets**	Michael Weeks	Rs. 350.00	452
8131800792	**Classical Electrodynamics**	Hans C. Dhanian	Rs. 395.00	620
8131800512	**The Software Vulnerability Guide**	Herbert H. Thompson, Scott G. Chase	Rs. 195.00	368
8131800776	**Robot Modelling and Kinematics**	Rachid Manseur	Rs. 295.00	380
8131800369	**System Software**	M. Joseph	Rs. 95.00	185
	STRAIGHT TO THE POINT SERIES			
8170084601	**STTP : Word 2002**	Corinne Hervo	Rs. 45.00	154
817008461X	**STTP : Excel 2002**	Corinne Hervo	Rs. 45.00	153
8170084628	**STTP : Dreamweaver 4**	Corinne Hervo	Rs. 45.00	135
8170084636	**STTP : Flash 5**	Corinne Hervo	Rs. 45.00	183
8170084644	**STTP : Photoshop 6**	Corinne Hervo	Rs. 45.00	152
817008881X	**STTP : MS Office 2000**	Dinesh Maidasani	Rs. 125.00	290
8170086100	**STTP : MS Office 2003**	Dinesh Maidasani	Rs. 145.00	288
8170087651	**STTP : MS Word 2003**	Firewall Media	Rs. 60.00	150
8170088011	**STTP : Photoshop CS**	Firewall Media	Rs. 60.00	150
8170088143	**STTP : MS Excel 2003**	Firewall Media	Rs. 60.00	150
8170088151	**STTP : CorelDraw 12**	Firewall Media	Rs. 60.00	150
8131800105	**STTP : 3ds MAX 7**	Dinesh Maidasani	Rs. 95.00	182
8131800083	**STTP : Auto CAD 2006**	Dinesh Maidasani	Rs. 95.00	190
8131800245	**STTP : CorelDraw X3**	Dinesh Maidasani	Rs. 75.00	188

Please write for a free color Firewall Media Catalog for details on the above books.

ISBN	TITLE	AUTHOR	PRICE	PAGES
8131800253	**STTP : Dreamweaver 8**	Dinesh Maidasani	Rs. 75.00	148
8131800237	**STTP : Photoshop CS2**	Dinesh Maidasani	Rs. 75.00	172
8170088380	**STTP : Tally 7.2**	Firewall Media	Rs. 175.00	322
8131800091	**STTP : Flash 8**	Dinesh Maidasani	Rs. 95.00	180
8131800407	**STTP : My SQL 5.0**	Dinesh Maidasani	Rs. 85.00	166
8131800458	**STTP : Microsoft Power Point 2003**	Dinesh Maidasani	Rs. 75.00	142

STUDIO FACTORY

ISBN	TITLE	AUTHOR	PRICE	PAGES
8170084792	**Studio Factory—Photoshop 6**	Christophe Aubry	Rs. 175.00	364
8170084806	**Studio Factory—Flash 5**	Sami Ben Yahiya	Rs. 145.00	314
8170084814	**Studio Factory—Dreamweaver Ultradev 4**	Phillippe Chatellier	Rs. 95.00	240
8170084822	**Studio Factory—Dreamweaver 4**	Christophe Aubry	Rs. 175.00	373
8170087643	**Studio Factory—Dreamweaver MX**	Christophe Aubry	Rs. 195.00	407
8170087627	**Studio Factory—Flash MX**	Arnaud Blanche	Rs. 145.00	337
817008766X	**Studio Factory—Photoshop 7**	Cyril Guerin	Rs. 195.00	420

LAXMI PUBLICATIONS (P) LTD

113, Golden House, Daryaganj, New Delhi-110002
Phone : **011 - 43 53 25 00**
Fax : **011 - 43 53 25 28**
EMAIL : info@laxmipublications.com
Website : www.laxmipublications.com

BRANCHES

- 129/1, IIIrd Main Road, IX Cross, Chamrajpet, **Bangalore** (*Phone* : 080-26 61 15 61)
- 26, Damodaran Street, T. Nagar, **Chennai** (*Phone* : 044-24 34 47 26)
- 43/1394D, St. Benedict's Road, Ernakulam North, **Cochin** (*Phone* : 0484-239 70 04)
- Pan Bazar, Rani Bari, **Guwahati** (*Phones* : 0361-254 36 69, 251 38 81)
- 4-2-453, Ist Floor, Ramkote, **Hyderabad** (*Phone* : 040-24 75 02 47)
- Adda Tanda Chowk, N.D. 365, **Jalandhar City** (*Phone* : 0181-222 12 72)
- 106/A, Ist Floor, S.N. Banerjee Road, **Kolkata** (*Phones* : 033-22 27 37 73, 22 27 52 47)
- 18, Madan Mohan Malviya Marg, **Lucknow** (*Phone* : 0522-220 95 78)
- 142-C, Victor House, Ground Floor, N.M. Joshi Marg, Lower Parel (W), **Mumbai** (*Phones* : 022-24 91 54 15, 24 92 78 69)
- Radha Govind Street, Tharpagna, **Ranchi** (*Phone* : 0651-230 77 64)